SPHERE COLOUR PLANT GUIDES
PESTS, DISEA[...]
IDENTIFIC[...]

G000108958

SPHERE BOOKS LIMITED
30-32 Gray's Inn Road, London WCIX 8JL

CONTENTS

INTRODUCTION

If you could place a giant magnifying glass over your garden it would most likely resemble an horrific battleground with phalanxes of extraordinary animals gnawing, chewing and sucking away at your plants and at one another.

Elsewhere a tide of multi-coloured diseases can threaten to over-run those plants which survive the onslaught of the insects.

BROWN ROT ON PLUM

It's war out there. The only way that the gardener can triumph is to summon up re-inforcements. In the battle of the herbaceous border and the vegetable plot the gardener's allies come in a variety of forms from chemical treatments to sound gardening technique and from natural cures to bio-logical controls which cunningly turn insect upon insect.

That is what this book is all about. The secret of fighting the war lies in ensuring that the punishment fits the crime. No general would dream of employing his big guns to quell a minor skirmish and, similarly, there is often no need to start pumping vast quantities of chemicals into your garden when a few simple gardening techniques will do.

The reverse of the coin, however, is that a good many gardeners waste valuable time, effort and money fighting the wrong battle. Failure to correctly identify the enemy and to give it the necessary drastic treatment can lead to the garden being over-run.

In this book we will be helping you to identify a vast range of garden pests and diseases, showing you how to identify their symptoms and telling you how best to control the problems.

So what are pests and diseases?

4

PESTS

These come in all shapes and sizes but for the purposes of this book we shall ignore the larger ones like rabbits and birds and deal with the smaller ones which cause by far the greatest problem. Generally they fall into five categories.

Chewers, like the pea and bean weevils and the turnip flea can strip a healthy leaf-blade overnight by simply eating their way through.

Suckers, like the capsid bug, the froghopper and the leaf-hopper attack plants by sucking out the juices in them, causing the foliage to shrivel up and die.

Red spiders, or mites, usually appear on the underside of the leaves. They can be observed best through a magnifying glass, feeding voraciously on the sap. They can be quite devastating particularly if they go un-noticed for a while.

Caterpillars, feed from the outer edges of the leaves working their way inwards. The commonest include the cabbage white butterfly and the tortrix moth.

Soil pests, generally the larvae of insects, which when adult are relatively harmless, can all be death to healthy plants. Leatherjackets, wire-worms, eelworms and all the other soil pests can cause whole sections of plants to just wither and die once the larvae have got control.

DISEASES

Most of the diseases affecting plants are fungal. They thrive in humid atmospheres, gen-erally, and enter through exposed wounds in the plants caused either by insects or by man. They can usually be effectively treated by fungi-cides or by improving the growing conditions.

If the diseases are not fungal, however, they may be more of a problem.

Bacterial diseases can be difficult to control. Usually the most effective form of action is cutting away the diseased parts of the plant and destroying them. Sometimes you will have to destroy the whole plant to avoid spreading.

Viral diseases will usually be beyond the means of the amateur gardener to control. They are frequently spread by aphids and other insects and treatments will usually concentrate on getting rid of the carriers. Plants affected by viral diseases will generally have to be destroyed.

YELLOW VIRUS APHID TRANSMITTED

You will see from this short pre-amble that regular inspection of your plants can be critical. Spot the problem in time and you may save the plant. Leave the infestation or the disease too long and your problems will be much greater.

Inspection with the naked eye must be done regularly and as soon as you spot a symptom which gives you case for concern closer inspection may be needed.

Some pests and diseases can only be properly identified by use of a magnifying glass. Clues to problems can be discolouration, weakening of the plant, early leaf-fall etc. Any or more of such symptoms can give clues to the problem.

The central section of this book gives you a comprehensive list of pests, diseases and weeds with colour pictures and a description to help you identify them. There are also details of the symptoms which give you clues to their presence, and full details of the treatments necessary to eradicate the problem.

The index section at the back gives you an invaluable aid in cross-referencing between the disease and the plant. If your problem lies with an apple tree, for instance, then look up Apple and it will give you a list of the commoner diseases affecting the apple tree. These can then be looked up in the central section for more information on treatments.

Elsewhere in this book there are chapters which give information on garden hygiene, natural methods of keeping down diseases like crop rotation and spacing, how to select healthy plants, what chemicals to buy and how to use them, equipment, biological controls and much more.

CHEMICALS

A considerable amount of time and money can be spent using chemicals in the garden when the return on that investment may not be properly justified. Chemicals should be considered as just one of a number of lines of attack. If good gardening techniques and natural remedies fail — and if the return in terms of crops will outweigh the cost of the chemicals and materials — then they should be called into battle. But it would be unwise to use chemicals as the universal panacea for all gardening problems — they are one section, important but not pre-eminent, in the gardener's battle against the tide of pests and diseases.

Garden hygiene, soil improvement, crop rotation, good cultural techniques and the use of biological controls — these can all have a part to play.

The use of chemicals must be integrated into the overall gardening pattern.

However, there are occasions when using chemicals is the only way to control some problems.

There are a vast number of chemical treatments with different compositions, uses and effects. Contact sprays like Derris will affect the insect itself. Ovicides like DNOC and tar-oil washes kill the eggs. Both of these only take effect on contact with the plant and so must cover all the plant surfaces.

Systemic insecticides like dimethoate and formothion are taken up through the roots and into the sap. They are useful for attacking the insects that suck the sap.

Most fungicides are designed to check or prevent attack and should therefore be applied as preventive treatments before diseases appear.

Some of the new part-systemic insecticides like benomyl are only effective for short periods.

Fungicides. Modern fungicides are safer to use than the old ones which were based on ingredients like copper, mercury and sulphur. In addition they are generally systemic which means that they can be absorbed by the roots of the plant and transmitted to the leaves in the sap stream. This does mean, however, that they cannot work in the other direction. This can inhibit their use and it has been found that some fungi have developed a natural resistance to many of the compounds found in them. The rule is always to try and find another type. If one fungicide doesn't work another may.

Insecticides. Some insecticides are systemic and thus pose less of a threat to parasites and predators since they are contained in the sap of the plant. Generally, insecticides are made in varying strengths and careful attention will need to be paid to the formulation of the dosage which will be clearly printed on the side of the container.

Most non-toxic insecticides will be non-selective in their action and will therefore be harmful to predators and beneficial insects alike so beware if they are not systemic. None of these should be sprayed onto open flowers, especially those on fruit trees, because this would result in the death of bees and thus reduce pollination.

Wound sealants. These should always be used to treat plant wounds whether caused during pruning or in any other way. A plant wound is an open invitation to attack and the wound sealant, if it contains a fungicide, will help to prevent the entry of unwanted disease. Those without a fungicide are of little use.

WARNING. Follow the manufacturers instructions to the letter when applying chemicals. Pay particular regard to the instructions about intervals between spraying and harvesting. Pests can develop immunity to some chemicals so if one treatment doesn't work try another. Do not spray indiscriminately in a high wind — you run the risk of damaging other plants and the predators which can do so much of the work for you by killing unwelcome pests.

Keep all chemicals safe and out of the reach of children and domestic pets. Make sure all bottles are properly labelled and don't transfer chemicals from one container to another. Try to spray on dull, still, dry days. Always wear rubber gloves. Mix only as much spray as you expect to need and flush any surplus down the lavatory. Dispose of all empty containers by capping them tightly, wrapping them in polythene and placing them in the dustbin. When spraying edible crops you must always allow the recommended interval before eating. When spraying is over wash your face and hands — especially after using pesticides or fungicides.

Remember, too, that chemicals have side-effects. Spray your apple tree with an anti-mildew fungicide and it will, indeed, help to ward off mildew but it may also kill off some of the pollen and thus reduce your crop. The message is clear — using chemicals should be carefully considered. Only use them when there is a clear and obvious need.

APPLICATION

The way in which a pesticide or fungicide is applied will depend on the form in which you buy it.

Sprays. These will be either liquid or soluble powders. Both are diluted with water and should be applied with a hand-sprayer or pump-up pressurised type of sprayer or, when suitable, a garden watering can with a fine rose sprinkler head.

Aerosols. These are cans of spray which have already been mixed. While usually more expensive they can be safer and easier to use especially with only a small number of plants. Shake before use and hold at the recommended distance from the plants. Do not allow the empty can to puncture.

Baits. Usually slug pellets.

These take the form of a poison bait which tempts the pests (slugs or snails). Group together and protect from rain and domestic animals.

Fumigants. These are usually used in the greenhouse to control pests. They take the form of smoke canisters or pellets. Close all the windows and light the pellet in the way you would a firework. Leave to smoulder, usually overnight. In the morning you can open the windows and ventilate the greenhouse.

Dust. These usually come in so-called "puffer-packs", rather like the material you use to clean the lavatory. Dusts should be applied to plants in a way which gives them a fine coating all over the foliage. Can look dirty and are, obviously, visible to the pests.

Granules. Usually used as slow-release soil insecticides to kill off pests which live, and overwinter, in the soil. Can be scattered on the soil from a dispenser. Some foliar insecticides nowadays come in the form of soluble granules which are simply dropped in water. Here is a guide to the commonest problems and the method of treatment.

Aphids suck the sap and so need to be attacked with a systemic insecticide.

Caterpillars chew leaves and so need to be attacked with a contact insecticide.

Mildew is a fungus which attacks and weakens leaves and stems and should be treated with a systemic fungicide.

Slugs eat plants and need to be killed with poisoned bait.

Soil pests eat roots and stems and so need to be attacked with dusts or granules which can get into the soil.

Virus diseases have no really effective treatment and the plants will usually have to be destroyed.

A GUIDE TO SOME COMMON PESTICIDES & FUNGICIDES

Bordeaux Mixture. A fungicide especially good against potato disease. Purchased as a powder ready for solution.

Bromophos. Soil insecticide used for control of cutworms, leatherjackets and wireworms. Available as a dust. Rake into soil.

Calomel. The commercial name for mercurous chloride. Kills the larvae of cabbage root fly and onion fly. Also used to control lawn diseases and check club root and onion white rot. Available as a dust.

Captan. A fungicide especially good for controlling apple and pear scab and rose black spot. Also used in seed dressings to protect against damping-off and other soil-borne diseases. It is available as a powder.

Cheshunt Compound. Soil fungicide used to control damping-off disease, collar-rot and other soil-borne diseases.

Derris. An insecticide effective against a range of pests including aphids, leaf-hoppers, thrips, caterpillars, apple-blossom weevil, pea and bean weevil, raspberry beetle, gooseberry sawfly, flea beetles and red spider mites. Available as a dust or a liquid. Leave a day before harvesting edible crops.

Diazinon. An insecticide used to kill aphids, capsid bugs, leaf miners, thrips, red spider mites, mealy bugs, scale insects and mushroom flies. Available as a liquid, in granular form or as a powder.

Dichlofluanid. A fungicide used mainly to control botrytis on fruit, and black spot on roses. At least two weeks must elapse before harvesting edible crops. Available as a powder.

Dinocap. A fungicide used mainly against powdery mildews but also for control of red spider mites. Available as a liquid or powder. Edible crops should not be harvested for at least one week.

DNOC. An insecticide which is added to petroleum oil to produce a winter wash for fruit trees to protect against over wintering of capsid bugs, apple suckers, aphids, winter moth, caterpillar, tortrix moth, red spider mites etc. Applied as a spray while trees are dormant.

Fenitrothion. Insecticide used against numerous pest including aphids, capsids, thrips, codling moth, sawflies, caterpillars and weevils. Available as a liquid. Edible crops should not be harvested for two weeks after application.

HCH. An insecticide used wet or dry and in smokes. Dusts are used against ants, earwigs, flea beetles, leatherjackets, wireworms etc. Sprays are used against all these plus aphids, apple suckers, cabbage root fly, capsid bugs, sawflies, thrips and woolly aphid. Don't harvest edible crops for two weeks after use.

Malathion. An insecticide used against a range of pests including aphids, leafhoppers, thrips, suckers, scale insects, mealy bugs, leaf miners, whiteflies, gooseberry sawfly, raspberry beetle and red spider mites. Available as an aerosol, dust or spray. Leave four days before harvesting edible crops.

Maneb. A fungicide used against downy mildews, rose black spot, potato blight, tomato leaf mould and tomato stem rot. Available as a powder. Leave one week before harvesting edible crops.

Pyrethrum. An insecticide which acts quickly against many insects including aphids, capsid bugs, leaf hoppers and thrips. Not always completely effective. Available as a dust, liquid and spray.

Tar oil wash. These are sprays made from tar distillate and used to clear fruit trees of aphid eggs, scale insects, caterpillar eggs, lichens and mosses. Applied when trees are dormant.

Thiram. A fungicide used to control a wide range of diseases including grey mould, rust, apple and pear scab, downy mildew, tomato leaf mould and some soil-borne diseases like damping-off and pea foot rot. Available as a dust and as a powder.

Trichlorphon. An insecticide used in killing flies, fly larvae, leaf miners, caterpillars, cutworms, earwigs and ants. Allow at least two days before harvesting edible crops.

Zineb. A fungicide used to protect against many diseases including potato blight, tomato leaf mould, mildew, rust, leaf spot and grey mould. Leave a week before harvesting edible crops.

WEEDS

The term "weed" is often applied to a number of plants which can give you an attractive, useful and certainly unusual addition to your garden.

Most dictionary definitions of the word weed rely upon descriptions like "useless", "troublesome" and "in-vasive". But even the most troublesome and invasive of plants, like the nettle, can have a number of uses i.e. in medicinal preparations and in attracting butterflies to the garden.

The answer lies with the individual. Get rid of those you don't want and retain the ones you do. But think twice about the wholsesale destruction of wild plants like daisies, Scarlet Pimpernel, wild pansies etc. Move them if they are in the way and restrict their growth with slates buried in the soil if they are invasive.

Try and adopt the attitude that some weeds are merely wild flowers growing in the wrong place.

The thoughtless destruction of wild flowers is slowly removing vast numbers of attractive plants from the landscape. It would be a tragedy if they were to disappear without trace.

However, it would be very hard to think of perennial weeds like couch grass, docks, ground elder and many nettles as charming wild additions to the garden.

Annual weeds like Chickweed, Shepherd's Purse and Groundsel are hardly a delight for the gardener who has to hoe and dig his way through them in order to establish a vegetable plot or herbaceous border.

If true weeds are not properly controlled they will give the gardener a nightmare and may mean that he has to leave his garden fallow in order to apply a destructive, blitz treatment.

There are two main ways of getting rid of weeds.

The hard-but-cheap way.

There is little point in spending time and money planting vegetables and flowers in a garden and then to have jungle of weeds compete with them for food and water and eventually over-running the crops. Both annual and perennial weeds are relatively easy to control in a garden which has been properly cultivated over a number of years. The real problem comes with a garden which has been neglected or which has been unattended for a number of years.

In that case the garden is likely to be populated by some pretty pernicious weeds. The worst of which will be perennials which multiply by sturdy rhizomes — those creeping underground stems that throw out numbers of new shoots without you being aware until they sprout up all over the garden.

A plot like this will need to be very thoroughly dug, probably using a double-spit method which really allows you to get to the roots of the weeds. Remove and burn every single trace. Even the smallest splinters of rhizome can produce new shoots.

Once a plot has been thoroughly dug the most serious problems should have been removed. From now on your weeding will consist largely of an attack on the familiar annuals. Hoe regularly, at least once every week, from April to July. Make a habit of doing this and you will find that these few minutes each week will save you painful hours clearing an overgrown plot later on. Put all annual weeds on the compost heap.

You will also need to do some hand-weeding on the fringes of growing plants where hoeing may threaten the established plants.

If you do find perennials returning near growing plants then loosen the soil with a trowel and remove the weed, roots and all. Burn them. Never put on the compost heap.

Mulching can help keep down weeds around crops and so, too, can the use of black polythene sheets.

The easy-but-expensive way.

Chemical weedkillers will

usually do the job most effectively as long as you use the right ones. There are three main types of chemical weedkillers.

Pre-emergence weedkillers. These are ones which inhibit the germination of weeds in order to give plants a better start. Propachlor is one example — it can be applied before sowing vegetables like leeks, brassicas and onions and will inhibit the germination of weeds for about six weeks.

Selective weedkillers. These, as the name suggests, kill weeds without harming the crop. One example is 2,4,5-T which can be used on nettles and thistles without killing the grass which may be around them.

Total weedkillers. These are very powerful but, as with Sodium Chlorate, can destroy everything nearby as well. Fortunately some have been developed, like paraquat/diquat which are contact weedkillers and which are rendered inactive on contact with the soil. These can be used on weeds and as long as they don't come into contact with plant foliage, won't damage nearby crops or flowers.

Perhaps the most useful weedkiller for the tenacious weeds is glyphosphate. Spray it on couch grass and elder — it moves effectively within the plants. With nettles cut them down and spray when they start to grow again.

Glyphosphate can also be effective in keeping weeds in check in an established garden. Glyphosphate gels are available which allow you to spot-treat weeds by brushing them, enabling you to attack weeds without risking damage to your growing plants.

Weed	Reproduction	Treatment
Bindweed	creeping rhizomes	Spot treat 2,4-D, paraquat/diquat
Buttercup (creeping)	seeds & runners	Spot treat 2,4-D, paraquat/diquat
Couch grass	rhizomes	Dalapon, paraquat/diquat, glyphosphate
Dock	seeds & rootstock	Spot treat 2,4-D, mecoprop
Dandelion	seeds & taproot	Spot treat 2,4-D, mecoprop
Ground Elder	rhizomes	2,4-D, 2,4,5-T, glyphosphate
Groundsel	seeds	hoeing, weeding
Horsetail	spores & rhizomes	2,4-D
Nettle	rhizomes & seeds	2,4-D, 2,4,5-T
Shepherd's Purse	seeds	hoeing, weeding
Thistle (creeping)	rhizomes	2,4-D, mecoprop, paraquat/diquat
Yellow Cress	stems & seeds	dichlobenil, paraquat/diquat

WEEDS IN LAWNS

A lawn means different things to different people. Some like a perfect, billiard-top, lawn with no intruders. Others are happy to see daisies, buttercups and other wild plants, which are often nowadays called weeds, in their lawn. It is a matter of choice.

Some lawn weeds do need to be controlled. They compete with the grass for food, moisture and space and can create conditions favourable for pests and diseases. Perhaps the answer lies in creating a happy medium.

There are two main types of lawn weeds and, as with other garden weeds, these are the annuals and the perennials.

Annual (or biennial) weeds are quite common in new lawns but less so in established ones since they tend not to like regular mowing.

Perennials fall into two categories; rosette and mat (carpet) forming weeds. Rosette forming weeds include plantain, daisy, and dandelion. Carpet-forming weeds include clover and pearlwort. The rosette-forming weeds are usually less difficult to remove than the carpet-forming ones. The first step in controlling weeds is to ensure that a lawn site, when it is being prepared, is free from weeds which will later attack it. If turfing see that the turf is weed-free.

Newly-sown lawns can usually be hand-weeded but once they become established the weeds are better eased out with a weeding tool or kitchen knife. Fill up the holes with soil.

Regular mowing will help to keep annuals down. Make sure your grass box is attached to the mower and rake the creeping weeds before mowing so that they stand upright and can better be cut by the mower blades. Weedkillers can be applied to lawns but make sure that you select a weedkiller suited to the purpose. Once again, before spraying, rake up the weeds so that the weedkiller attacks all the surfaces of the weeds. Apply evenly and, if spraying with a watering can, invest in a spray bar. Take care that the liquid isn't spread onto other plants — the lawn weedkillers may not affect the grass but that might not apply to nearby flowers. Leave for three days before mowing and remember not to use the clippings for mulching. You can spot-treat isolated patches of weeds.

SOME COMMON WEEDKILLERS

Calomel.
Used as a mosskiller in liquid or powder form. Slow in action.

2,4-D.
A selective weedkiller which kills many lawn weeds without damaging grass. Also effective against bindweed. Harmful to most garden plants.

Dalapon.
Systemic weedkiller which kills grasses including couch grass, reeds and sedges. Sold as a powder.

Glyphosphate.
Systemic weedkiller which will kill most plants. Most effective when applied to plants in growth — especially young leaves. Kills roots, leaves and stems — even in deep-rooting weeds like bindweed, ground elder and docks.

Mecoprop.
Systemic selective weedkiller used to control weeds in lawns, especially clover.

Paraquat.
Total contact weedkiller rendered inactive on contact with soil. Becomes poisonous in the plant leaf by photosynthesis, thus light is essential for action. Extremely poisonous to all warm-blooded animals.

Sodium chlorate.
Total weedkiller used in clearing waste land and for paths and drives. Moves about in soil and can kill other plants. May remain for a long time in heavy soils.

BIOLOGICAL CONTROL

The larva of a ladybird can consume between 250 and 500 aphids. The adult can consume well over 500 aphids. If a ladybird can therefore consume over 1,000 aphids in its life-cycle it doesn't take a genius to work out how valuable the presence of ladybirds can be to the gardener.

The use of predators to keep garden pests under control has developed a good deal in recent years and though the commercial availability of them is still limited it will grow in the coming years.

In nature the insects which damage crops are kept under control by natural enemies, as we have seen with the ladybird, and the use of chemicals can often actually harm this process. Chemical insecticides can often do more damage to the natural predators than to the pests, many of which have developed some resistance to the chemicals.

In the garden this frail balance is difficult to maintain and the use of chemicals is often the only satisfactory approach.

However, in a carefully controlled environment like the greenhouse the introduction of biological controls is far more effective.

At present there are three main biological control agents which are available to the amateur gardener.

A small parasitic wasp (Encarsia formosa) which attacks the glasshouse whitefly; a predatory mite from Chile (Phytoseiulus persimilis) which kills the notorious red spider mites and a bacterium (Cryptolaemus montrouzieri) which introduces a killer disease into caterpillars.

Experiments are being conducted into a vast range of other biological control agents including a type of ladybird which feeds on mealybugs. It is an area which is expanding rapidly. The virtues of biological controls in the greenhouse can be simply stated:

Firstly, these natural enemies attack only the specific pests that they are introduced to kill. They die out once that has been achieved.

Secondly, they obviate the need for pesticides. Indeed, they will often be more sensitive to pesticides than the pests themselves and once biological controls are introduced the use of pesticides will have to be restricted to those recommended by the suppliers.

Thirdly, they are preventive rather than curative in that once pests or diseases have become rampant in the greenhouse they will not be much good. If introduced at the first sign of pests or disease they will, however, stop them in their tracks. This places a responsibility on the gardener to keep a regular check on his plants but gives him the ability to introduce a quick and effective control which will stop the spread of problems and safeguard his plants.

Finally, many pests — especially the whitefly and the spider mite — have developed a resistance to some pesticides. Biological controls may be the only effective way of tackling the problem.

One word of warning, however, the remains of pests may disfigure plants. Such biological controls may be best used on edible crops rather than ornamental ones.

GOOD GARDENING

Prevention is always better than the cure and the secret of reducing the invasion of pests and diseases lies in good gardening techniques.

Hygiene. Impetuosity can be death to plants. They resent constant handling and prodding. Let your cuttings grow and your young plants develop without delivering the kind of shock treatment from too frequent handling that will impede their growth and make them weak and vulnerable.

Ensure that your tools and pots are clean. Many diseases are introduced into plants from equipment that has been in contact with them elsewhere. See, too, that you don't overwater or overfeed your plants. Diseases flourish in damp conditions. Work in a good supply of organic matter like well-rotted manure to improve the nutritional value of the soil and its drainage.

Dig new soil thoroughly removing any weeds. Fertilisers applied at the rate of about two handfuls per square yard, scattered or hoed in, will replace the nutrients washed out of the soil by the winter rains. It will also help them to grow strong and resistant to pests and diseases.

In the summer you can spray a liquid feed onto the plant leaves but avoid feeding outdoors after the summer. This may promote sappy growth which will be unable to resist the ensuing frosts.

Light and Heat. Always select a site which gives the plant access to plenty of light. Most plants manufacture their food with the help of sunlight. Most also need warmth to grow. A minimum temperature of around 6C is needed before they will grow, so cold spots can lead to stunted growth and a late start which will force a delay in sowing seed. There are some exceptions to this rule — one or two plants will actually grow well in shady sites. Consult the growing advice on your seed packet. Spacing of plants is also very important, both to ensure that they get enough light and to see that they don't cluster together promoting unhealthy growing conditions which can be inviting to some pests and diseases.

Crop rotation. Soil which is used year after year for

growing the same plants can build-up micro-organisms, pests and diseases which will damage growth.

Brassicas, for instance, can be prone to the development of club-root if regularly grown on the same site. Tomatoes grown for more than a couple of years in unsterilised soil can develop root problems. The habit of growing the same plants in the same site can also deprive the soil of certain plant acids. A system of crop rotation can therefore be vital in promoting good, healthy and abundant growth. A typical three-year crop rotation scheme for a vegetable garden is given here to show you the idea.

Crop Rotation Plan

Divide your plot into three sections:–

YEAR 1	Section 1	Section 2	Section 3
,,	Lettuce	Tomatoes	Cabbage
,,	Peas	Carrots	Cauliflower
,,	Courgettes	Parsnip	Broccoli
,,	Beans	Turnip	Brussels Sprouts
,,	Cucumber	Swede	Kale
,,	Leeks	Sweetcorn	—
,,	Onions	Potatoes	—
,,	Radish	Beetroot	—
,,	Spinach	—	—
YEAR 2	As for Section 3	As for Section 1	As for Section 2
YEAR 3	As for Section 2	As for Section 3	As for Section 1

Healthy Plants. The best way to ward off pests and diseases is to make sure that your plants start out healthy. When buying plants check them thoroughly for any tell-tale signs of diseases or pests. Infected plants should be rejected — not only because of their inherent problems but because they will introduce the problem into your garden and infect other plants. Mottling and distortion are signs of virus infection. Check beneath the leaves of the plants for any bugs that might be resident there.

Some plants can be bought certified virus-free. They may be slightly more expensive but should guarantee you a healthy plant. You can also buy dressed seed which has been treated with chemicals that combat garden pests and diseases. Again this will be more expensive but will give you peace of mind.

The technique of breeding plants that have a natural resistance to pests and diseases has grown in recent years and is particularly applied to those plants where it has been found that control by chemical means is either undesirable or ineffective.

Among these are potatoes like Maris Peer and Pentland Crown which will resist attacks from potato blight. Arran Pilot and King Edward are varieties that have been bred to resist scab. Resistant rootstocks are now quite common, especially for tomatoes which are bred for resistance to virus diseases and leaf-mould. Lettuces which are resistant to mildew, and antirrhinums resistant to rust are other examples of specially developed rootstocks that can improve your plant growth. There are lots of others. Your stockist should be able to advise you on these.

WEATHER

If a plant shows unhealthy symptoms you should not automatically assume that the reason lies with pests and diseases. Plants can be badly affected by extremes of temperature and other weather conditions. Unfortunately, however, there are pests and diseases which enjoy almost all types of weather and will take advantage of the conditions.

Cold weather. Generally speaking, cold weather is a gardener's ally because it can remove over-wintering pests that might survive warmer weather. Unfortunately plant species respond differently to cold weather depending on whether they are hardy, half-hardy or tender. With soft or herbaceous plants wilting can happen followed by die-back. Splitting of bark may also occur though those plants with woody stems usually have a reserve of sap in the trunk and may not react to cold weather and the freezing of water supplies so quickly. Sudden thaws must also be watched out for. They can cause blackening of leaves and flowers and lead to Botrytis or soft rot. Any tissue damage caused by cold weather can create wounds through which pests and diseases can enter. If frosts persist into spring new growth may also be damaged. Drape fruit trees with muslin sacking or old net curtains to keep the frosts off new shoots.

Rain. Wet weather is ideal for slugs and snails — especially if the weather is warm. Poisoned bait placed under a propped-up tile or slate near the plant will attract considerable numbers of slugs and snails in this type of weather. Beware! This is poison and can be harmful to domestic pets. Rain can also cause the dampness that leads to fungal and other diseases. Check plants carefully.

Sun. Warm humid conditions are ideal for growing but they are also ideal for fungal activity. In the summer and in warm moist springs fungi can race through plants especially if they are planted too close together and the air cannot circulate freely. Space plants sensibly and prune. High temperatures also encourage the increased growth of aphids. Massive colonies can build up in a matter of days and fairly regular spraying will be necessary. Excess sun can also lead to the scorching and burning of some plants — especially those which in their natural conditions would grow in the shade or half shade i.e. large-leafed begonias.

Dry. The red spider mite and other mites — those free-breeding and tenacious pests common to fruit trees and greenhouses — love dry conditions. They can be highly destructive and regular treatment with insecticides will be needed. When conditions are dry, particularly in the greenhouse, spraying healthy plants with water twice a day can help to keep down mites.

Wind. High winds can destroy crops simply by blowing them down or uprooting them. Make sure all but the sturdiest plants are placed where they will not come into contact with strong winds. However, wind can also cause the browning of leaf margins especially in ornamental acers and other soft-leafed shrubs and trees.

PESTS

AN ALPHABETICAL GLOSSARY

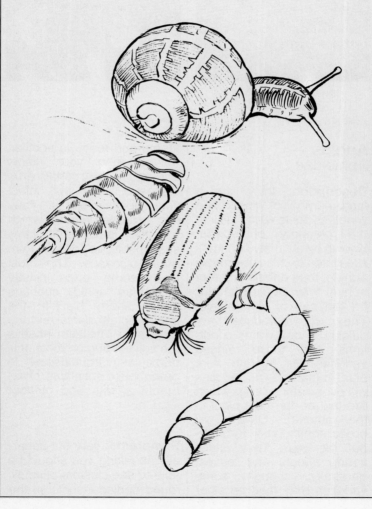

ROSE APHIDS

MEALY CABBAGE APHIDS

Aphids
Aphididae

Description: there are a large number of winged and wingless pests which fall into the category of aphids. Known by a variety of names like greenfly, blackfly, mealy aphids, rose aphids and root aphids they all feed heartily on the sap of your plants. They will reproduce very quickly under warm conditions and those winged varieties will migrate from plant to plant. Some varieties will overwinter as eggs which are laid on the host plant in the autumn. Others will breed continuously throughout the year. They attack young shoots and leaves, generally, though some varieties may feed on older stems and roots. In addition to attacking your plants aphids can carry certain virus diseases which will infect your healthy plants. They can also open wounds which will then leave your plants susceptible to attack from other diseases. The most troublesome forms include the bean aphid, cabbage aphid, cherry blackfly, the peach-potato aphid and the root aphid. The latter inhabits the soil feeding on roots. It is particularly troublesome in greenhouse pot plants, ornamental plants and outdoor lettuce.

Symptoms: vary but generally speaking you should be able to see clusters of small, round-bodied insects on the

APPLE APHIDS

BLACK APHIDS

leaves and stems of your plants. They come in a variety of colours. Some will cause extreme conditions of leaf curl. Some cause a distortion of the shoots, stems and flowers. Some will cause galls and swellings while others will infest the roots. Their sap-sucking habit, however, will cause a general weakening of all plants. Aphids also excrete a nasty sticky honeydew which builds up in sooty moulds on diseased plants weakening and disfiguring them. These sooty moulds tend to restrict the amount of light which reaches the leaves and therefore inhibits leaf development. Honeydew also attracts ants which feed on it and can spread aphids and other pests.

Treatment: there is a wide variety of insecticides available to control aphids but strengths, doses and frequency of usage vary from one to another. Read carefully the manufacturer's directions. Aphids can develop a resistance to treatments and it may be necessary to vary the insecticide occasionally to prevent this. On large shrubs and trees, and some herbaceous plants, it may be very difficult to fully control an aphid attack but continue doses to keep the spread in check. If the colonies are accessible then treatments like malathion, nicotine or bioresmethrin in spray form may be best. If they are not easy to get at then a systemic insecticide like dimethoate or

APHIDS IN SOIL

formothion will be best. You can also purchase dusts though these have to be applied powerfully to get at hidden colonies. Any over-wintering eggs on dormant fruit trees can be treated with tar oil or DNOC/petroleum.

Root aphids have to be treated differently. Drench infested root systems with a spray-strength solution of diazinon.

Apple sawfly
Hoplocampa testudinea

Description: resembling small flying ants they land on apple trees in spring laying eggs in the blossom. When hatched caterpillars bore into the fruit. At fruit-fall remain in soil until spring.

Symptoms: ribbon-like scars in the fruit, black messy deposit, unpleasant smelling fruit inclined to drop early.

Treatment: regular cultivation under trees destroys overwintering caterpillars. Destroy infested fruits. Spray with fenitrothion immediately after petalfall.

Asparagus beetle
Crioceris asparagi

Description: from early June onwards the adult beetles and the larvae feed on the young shoots and foliage. Severe attacks can completely strip plants.

Symptoms: adult beetles ¼-inch long visible on foliage. Black heads, red bodies, yellow spots on black wing cases. Eggs laid on shoots.

Treatment: hand-pick beetles from plants. Remove rubbish from beds in winter. Spray or dust with derris or gamma-HCH from June onwards.

Bulb scale mite
Steneotarsonemus laticeps

Description: microscopic mites which attack bulbs, especially amaryllis and narcissus. Like the warmth of a greenhouse and live between the bulb scales.

Symptoms: severe infestations cause rust-coloured streaks on stems and foliage. Stunting and distorted leaves on flowers. Stored bulbs appear soft and dry.

Treatment: destroy all bulbs infested. Chemical treatments are difficult. Try hot-water treatment. Dip dormant bulbs in water at 43°C for 4 hours. Can use thionazin as a bulb dip.

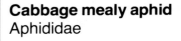

Cabbage mealy aphid
Aphididae

Description: one of the myriad varieties of aphid. Small and grey it is found on the undersides of cabbages feeding on the sap of young shoots. Can transmit viruses.

Symptoms: leaves turn yellow, aphid colonies visible by inspecting the undersides of leaves.

Treatment: destroy all crop debris at the end of the growing season. Spray with fenitrothion.

Cabbage root fly
Erioischia brassicae

Description: small white maggots of the fly live in the soil and attack the roots of cabbages and other brassicas.

Symptoms: affected plants will wilt, especially the younger ones which can be killed off completely. It is especially prevalent in dry weather. Adult flies lay eggs on or near stems at soil level.

Treatment: transplants and seedlings can be protected by mixing diazinon granules into soil around plants or by watering in a spray-strength solution of diazinon. Check attacks on established plants by drenching roots in spray strength mixture of diazinon.

Cabbage Whitefly
Aleyrodes proletella

Description: often not noticed until the plant is disturbed this is a pest which attacks cabbages, Brussels sprouts and other brassicas. Often active in winter when other insects are not.

Symptoms: small white flies flying off the leaves when disturbed. Checked plant growth. Discoloured, sticky leaves.

Treatment: spray with malathion or pyrethrum.

Capsid bugs
Capsidae

Description: a variety of bugs which includes the apple capsid bug, the common grey capsid bug and the bishop bug. All cause damage to a wide range of plants including apples, currants and herbaceous plants.

Symptoms: mis-shaped and discoloured fruits and ragged holes in young leaves. Buds and growing points die-off.

Treatment: overwinter in plant debris so remove it and burn. Spray in winter with DNOC/petroleum on deciduous hosts like apples. In summer spray ornamental plants only with fenitrothion or gamma-HCH. Regular doses.

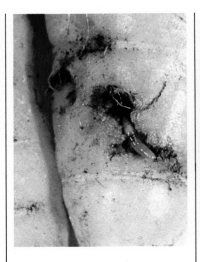

Carrot fly
Psila rosae

Description: a persistent pest which will need determined controlling. Small yellowish maggots feed on the roots of carrots, celery and parsnips.

Symptoms: young plants die-off and the roots of older plants are spoiled by extensive tunnelling.

Treatment: sow dressed seed thinly in May and when thinning burn the discarded seedlings. Scatter diazinon granules along the row. In autumn destroy all infested plants to kill off overwintering pupae. Water autumn carrots mid-August with spray-strength mixture of diazinon.

Caterpillars
Lepidoptera

Description: the larval stage of moths and butterflies. Eat leaves though some eat stems, roots and fruits. More than 50 species.

Symptoms: obvious from ragged, gnawed leaves. Heavy infestations can completely destroy plant.

Treatment: pick off by hand or spray with derris, malathion, trichlorphon or bioresmethrin.

Cockchafer
Melolontha melolontha

Description: one of a number of adult chafers which also include the summer chafer, rose chafer and garden chafer. They feed on leaves flowers and fruits. Larvae can seriously damage roots, bulbs, tubers and stems.

Symptoms: larvae identified from their fat, white bodies, distinct brown head and three pairs of legs.

Treatment: adult beetles controlled by gamma-HCH spray, larvae by treating soil with gamma-HCH dust or spray and by deep cultivation to expose them to predators.

Codling moth
Cydia pomonella

Description: it is the caterpillars of this small moth that do the damage burrowing into apples, pears and other fruit through the eyes.

Symptoms: maggoty apples. Hollow, brown and rotted cores which will often contain caterpillars.

Treatment: chemical control difficult. To be effective spray with fenitrothion in mid-June in the brief period between eggs hatching and the caterpillars reaching protection. Spray again 3 weeks later.

Eelworms
Nematoda

Description: a serious pest, despite its size, especially in herbaceous plants and vegetables. Thin, transparent, tiny worms resembling miniature eels. Increase rapidly.

Symptoms: discoloration and deformity of leaves and flowers. Plants affected will usually die.

Treatment: no effective chemical treatment exists. Destroy infested plants.

Froghoppers
Cercopidae

Description: otherwise known as froth-flies these pests, especially when young, feed on the plant sap of lavender, chrysanthemum, roses and other plants.

Symptoms: masses of froth, commonly known as cuckoo-spit, on stems. Distorted young growth.

Treatment: spray copiously with malathion, gamma-HCH or nicotine.

Gooseberry sawfly
Nematus species

Description: sawfly caterpillars feed on the leaves of gooseberries and currants causing severe damage, rapidly stripping plants of foliage.

Symptoms: leaves stripped and defoliated. Green, black-spotted caterpillars in May causing damage until September.

Treatment: spray with derris or nicotine in late spring or when caterpillars appear. Isolated attacks can be controlled by hand-picking caterpillars and destroying them.

Leaf Cutter Bee
Megachile species

Description: a pest which resembles a small, hairy hive bee. Seldom causes serious damage but continued attack can disfigure and weaken plants. Attacks roses, laburnum, syringa and other shrubby plants.

Symptoms: females attack by cutting semi-circular pieces out of leaves which are used to make thimble-shaped breeding cells.

Treatment: no proper chemical control. Locate and destroy nests in soil, decaying wood or old brickwork.

 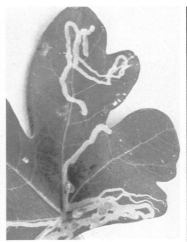

Leafhoppers
Cicadellidae

Description: small insects which are related to aphids and feed on the sap of a wide variety of plants both outdoors and under glass.

Symptoms: when disturbed these green insects can be seen leaping from the undersides of the foliage — thus their name. Light mottling on surface of leaves, skin-casts left attached.

Treatment: damage will usually be slight but they can transmit virus diseases. Control by spraying with malathion or nicotine every two weeks.

Leaf Miners

Description: a variety of moth and fly larvae which burrow into the leaves of plants. They include Columbine leaf-miner (phytomyza aquilegiae), laburnum leaf-miner (leucoptera laburnella) and lilac leaf-miner (caloptilia syringella).

Symptoms: mining or tunnelling in leaves. Varies from simple blotching to extensive sinuous tunnels.

Treatment: chemical control not always necessary if attacks are mild. If damage is persistent however spray with gamma-HCH, diazinon or pirimiphos-methyl.

Leatherjacket
Tipulidae

Description: grubs which have soft but tough skins, they are the fat, legless larvae of crane-flies. They feed on roots of a wide-range of plants. Especially troublesome on lawns. Live in the soil.

Symptoms: can kill whole patches of grass and cause wilting and death of ornamental plants and vegetables.

Treatment: deeply cultivate soil to expose grubs to birds. Protect individual plants by scattering bromophos or diazinon granules in the soil. Water turf with gamma-HCH solution in autumn.

Mealybugs
Pseudococcidae

Description: a serious problem in greenhouses these pests particularly enjoy grape vines and in the warmth can breed through the year. Adult females resemble small woodlice.

Symptoms: they excrete honeydew which leaves sooty moulds on leaves and stems.

Treatment: spray with diazinon or malathion before fruit starts to swell. Further sprays every 2 weeks. Use tar oil on dormant deciduous plants.

Mites
Acarina

Description: small, some-times microscopic, they are related to spiders and are commonly called red spider mites. Vast range of mites — many cause considerable damage.

Symptoms: bleaching, mottl-ing and yellowing of leaves. Thick webs which shelter colonies of mites visible beneath leaves. May need a magnifying glass.

Treatment: too well protect-ed for chemical treatment to succeed. Destroy all infested plants.

Millipedes
Diplopoda

Description: distinguished from centipedes by their greater number of legs, grey/black colouring and their slower movement. A problem in greenhouses and in root crops.

Symptoms: tunnelling in potatoes and other root crops.

Treatment: good garden hygiene and deep cultivation of the soil, especially if it is damp. Plenty of organic material in soil.

 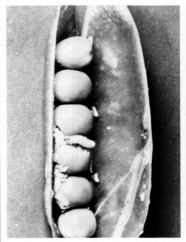

Onion Fly
Delia antiqua

Description: one of the most serious pests infesting onions, shallots and leeks. The maggots are white and legless and tunnel into plant tissue especially when young.

Symptoms: yellowing of leaves, withered and musty bulbs, rotting tissue.

Treatment: before sowing apply calomel dust to soil. Spray with trichlorpon 2 or 3 times in May and June. It is attracted by the scent of crushed onion leaves so clear and burn waste and thinnings.

Pea Moth
Laspeyresia nigricans

Description: probably the most serious pest attacking peas. The caterpillar commonly found in pea pods is that of the Pea Moth. Eggs laid in June, July, August.

Symptoms: pale-yellow caterpillars inside pods feeding.

Treatment: spray with fenitrothion as flowers open. Grow early maturing varieties which are harvested in mid-July or late-maturing, sown after mid-June.

Scale insects
Coccidae

Description: related to mealy bugs these insects are inclined to be troublesome on house plants and in the greenhouse — especially on vines and peaches.

Symptoms: yellow or brown scales beneath leaves. Young insects swarm all over plants feeding and excreting honeydew. Black sooty moulds.

Treatment: spray with malathion or diazinon especially when they are hatching. May need systemic insecticide like dimethoate or formothion.

Slugs
Arion species

Description: at least six different types likely to attack garden plants. Feed at night and hide in debris, under boxes, stones or plants.

Symptoms: eat holes in leaves, stems buds and flowers above ground and roots, tubers and bulbs below ground. Slime trails indicate movement.

Treatment: slug pellets scattered under plants. Metaldehyde watered onto plants and soil or added to bait like bonemeal. Pick off slugs.

Swift Moth
Hepialidae

Description: the caterpillars of these moths live in soil and show when you dig it over. Feed on the roots of both cultivated plants and weeds.

Symptoms: dirty-white caterpillars with brown heads. 1–2 ins. long.

Treatment: good garden hygiene and cultivation. Work bromophos, diazinon granules or gamma-HCH dust into surrounding soil.

Tortrix moth
Tortricidae

Description: the caterpillars of these moths feed on the roots of a wide variety of cultivated plants. They differ from other caterpillars by spinning webs used to draw in plant material on which they feed.

Symptoms: holes in leaves, silky threads around leaves, stems, fruits and flowers. Small caterpillars visible.

Treatment: pick off caterpillars by hand. Chemical control difficult but forceful spraying with pirimiphos-methyl, derris or trichlorphon may be effective.

Whitefly
Aleyrodidae

Description: the adult whitefly, sometimes known as the snowfly, looks rather like a minute white moth but is closely related to aphids and scale insects.

Symptoms: the whitefly nymph lives beneath leaves, feeding on sap and excreting the characteristic honeydew making plants sticky and leaving familiar black sooty moulds.

Treatment: spray with pyrethrum or pirimiphos-methyl when adult whiteflies first observed.

Wasps
Vespidae

Description: troublesome in late summer and early autumn when they eat the ripening fruit of apples, pears and plums.

Symptoms: enlarged damage on fruit caused initially by birds and exacerbated by wasps. Wasps visible feeding on fruit.

Treatment: locate and destroy wasp nests. Place carbaryl dust in the entrance to the nest at dusk when most of the wasps will be inside.

Winter moth

Description: caterpillars which can cause considerable damage to the foliage of flowers and young fruits.

Symptoms: open flowers and young leaves holed or spun together. Green caterpillars may be observed. Plants likely to be attacked in spring.

Treatment: fasten Boltac grease band around tree trunks September to March to stop adult moths getting up tree and laying eggs. Spray with derris, fenitrothion or malathion as buds open.

Wireworm
Elateridae

Description: the tough and horny larvae of click beetles which feed in the soil on tubers, roots and stems of potatoes, lettuces and tomatoes.

Symptoms: yellow-brown, worm-like creatures with long, cylindrical shiny bodies and three pairs of legs. Observed on plant roots.

Treatment: gamma-HCH on infested soil but not among edible crops. For these use diazinon or bromophos powder. Regular cultivation of soil should remove them.

Wolly aphid
Eriosoma lanigerum

Description: a species of aphid which will commonly attack apple trees, other trees and shrubs. Infest twigs and branches. Can lead to die-back of shoots and branches.

Symptoms: tufts of white, waxy wool on twigs and branches. Continuous feeding on trees leads to woody galls. In summer colonies of aphids visible.

Treatment: chemical control difficult since they are too well protected in cracks and crevices. Brush a spray-strength solution of a systemic insecticide into colonies of aphids or spray strongly with malathion before bud burst and again after petal fall.

Vine weevil
Otiorhynchus sulcatus

Description: a species of weevil whose larvae damage the roots of plants like the rhododendron, cyclamen and begonia. Adults are small beetles, dark-coloured with a prolonged snout. Larvae are white legless grubs.

Symptoms: lower leaves eaten and left tattered. Weakened roots.

Treatment: spray with gamma-HCH or fenitrothion. A gamma-HCH seed dressing followed by gamma-HCH spray can be effective.

OTHER PESTS

Bean seed fly
Delia platura

Description: maggots which eat into the germinating seeds of beans, peas, sweetcorn and other vegetables.

Symptoms: small, white, legless maggots eating into the seeds.

Treatment: dress seed with gamma-HCH/Thiram before sowing.

Black currant gall mite
Cecidophyopsis ribis

Description: one of the most serious pest problems affecting black currants, not simply because of the damage it can do but because it can also transmit reversion virus which retards cropping.

Symptoms: buds swell up and fail to develop. This is the condition known as "big bud".

Treatment: control by spraying with a 1% solution of benomyl when flowers open and again three weeks later. Cut out and burn infested buds. Destroy any plants affected by reversion.

Bulb mite
Rhizoplyphus echinopus

Description: a mite which is unfortunately common in the soil and invades rotting tissue of bulbous plants like the narcissus, tulip and hyacinth.

Symptoms: small, pearly-white mites in the soil and on rotting bulbs.

Treatment: usually a secondary pest associated with eelworms and insects. Deal with the primary problem and it should not appear.

Celery fly
Philophylla heraclei

Description: maggots burrowing into the leaf tissue of celery and parsnips causing leaves to shrivel up and die if left unchecked.

Symptoms: brown blotches on the leaves. Retarded growth. Small, white leaf-mining maggots present in April and through to the summer.

Treatment: spray young plants with dimethoate, malathion or trichlorphon.

Chrysanthemum eelworm
Aphelenchoides ritzemabos

Description: one of the most serious pests to affect chrysanthemums, it can also attack other plants, notably China asters, paeonies and other ornamentals.

Symptoms: microscopic eelworms penetrate the tissue of the leaves and stems. Infested foliage turns brown or black between the main veins. Severe attacks can retard growth and kill plants.

Treatment: difficult to stop infestations that have become established. Good garden hygiene and healthy stock is the best answer. Dig up and burn infested plants.

Cutworms
Noctuidae

Description: cutworm is the name of the caterpillar of various species of moth which attack a range of plants especially root vegetables and lettuces.

Symptoms: green or greybrown fat caterpillars in the soil. Stems eaten at soil level and may be severed.

Treatment: thorough cultivation and good weed control. Treat soil with gamma-HCH, bromophos or diazinon granules.

Earwigs
Forficula auricularia

Description: young and adult earwigs can cause considerable damage especially to the blooms of chrysanthemums, clematis and dahlia. They will also feed on the leaves of these and other decorative plants. They feed at night.

Symptoms: ragged, gnawed edges and holes in petals and leaves.

Treatment: remove garden debris which provides shelter for the earwigs. Spray gamma-HCH or trichlorphon on and around infested plants.

Flea beetle
Phyllotreta species

Description: adult fly beetles afflict the seedlings of a wide range of plants including turnips, swedes, cabbages and wallflowers.

Symptoms: the pests gnaw small holes, circular in shape, in the seedlings and in young leaves. Active on sunny days. Severe attacks will badly impede growth.

Treatment: good garden hygiene. Dust seedlings with derris or carbaryl.

Gall midges
Cecidomyiidae

Description: the adult gall midge is a small fly measuring no more than one tenth of an inch. It feeds on plant tissue in stems, leaves and flowers in a vast range of cultivated plants.

Symptoms: small, bright red, yellow or white maggots.

Treatment: the larvae are usually protected by the galls and so are not easily reached by insecticides. Persistant spraying with gamma-HCH. Aim to kill adults before they lay eggs in late spring/early summer.

Mangold fly
Pegomya betae

Description: a small fly whose maggots tunnel into the leaves of spinach and beetroot.

Symptoms: damaged leaves will turn brown and wither. Severe attacks of the mangold fly maggot will retard plant growth.

Treatment: spray with dimethoate formothion or trichlorphon as soon as you spot the problem. Usually from May onwards.

Mushroom flies

Description: the maggots of a number of species of fly eat into the stalks and the caps of mushrooms making them inedible.

Symptoms: visible clusters of small adult flies on the mushrooms. Tunnels created by the maggots.

Treatment: spray infested mushroom beds with malathion or nicotine.

Mustard beetle
Phaedon cochleariae

Description: adult beetles and their larvae feed on the leaves and stems of mustard, watercress, cabbages, swedes and turnips. Active from May onwards. Infestations can be severe in August.

Symptoms: adult beetles are metallic blue. Larvae are brownish yellow.

Treatment: malathion dust or sprays. Don't use if growing cress in streams or rivers as it will kill fish and contaminate the river. Raise water level to drown beetles and larvae.

Narcissus fly
Merodon equestris

Description: a serious pest affecting daffodils killing the bulbs or causing flower failure. Smaller narcissus flies are also found on a wide range of bulbs as secondary pests invading tissue that has already rotted after attack from pests like eelworms, slugs and snails.

Symptoms: flower failure, grass-like leaves and soft, short maggots infesting bulbs.

Treatment: no effective chemical control. Regular cultivation of the soil around the bulbs will help to discourage females laying eggs. Cover bulbs with soil in May and June which is the most active period of the flies. Immerse dormant bulbs in gamma-HCH mixture.

Potato cyst eelworm
Globodera species

Description: one of the most serious pests attacking potatoes and also affecting tomatoes. Soil-borne pests invade the root system retarding plant growth and in serious infestations causes plants to collapse and die.

Symptoms: young eelworms are hatched out from eggs and are protected by tough brown cysts. Each cyst can contain several hundred eggs which fall to the soil and can remain dormant for several years.

Treatment: no effective chemical control. Crop rotation and good garden hygiene. Deeply cultivated soil around plants disturbs dormant eggs. Sterilise soil.

Pea thrips
Kakothrips robustus

Description: small elongated insects that attack the leaves of peas and broad beans in June and July.

Symptoms: leaves and pods show a silver mottling. Severe infestations can lead to stunted growth, limited flowering and poor pod production.

Treatment: examine plants carefully from June onwards. Spray or dust with fenitrothion or malathion.

Raspberry beetle
Byturus tomentosus

Description: small beetle whose grubs tunnel into the young fruits of the raspberry, loganberry and blackberry.

Symptoms: distorted fruit infested with maggots. Attacks June to August.

Treatment: destroy grubs before they enter fruits. Spray with derris, fenitrothion or malathion as flowering ends and again when fruits begin to colour.

Strawberry beetle
Pterostichus species

Description: ground beetles which bite into ripening strawberries causing considerable damage and crop loss.

Symptoms: black, shiny beetles which can be seen scuttling about under affected trusses of fruit. Can be confused with bird or slug damage.

Treatment: keep beds weed-free. Control beetles with methiocarb pellets.

Suckers
Psyllidae

Description: related to aphids, these pests can be distinguished from them by their flattened bodies, large eyes and wing-buds. Feed on plant sap.

Symptoms: infested plants have foul, sticky excretion on them which results in distorted growth. Apple suckers infest blossom trusses and over-winter as eggs laid in trees in the autumn. Pear suckers overwinter as adults, laying eggs in mid-March.

Treatment: spray apple suckers with winter spray of tar-oil or DNOC/petroleum. Spray pear suckers with dimethoate, formothion or malathion after petal fall.

Weevils
Curculionidae

Description: a wide range of weevils attack plants from the adults, generally dark with a prolonged snout, to the larvae which are usually white, legless grubs.

Symptoms: feed on the roots, tubers, corms, leaves, flowers, fruits and stems. Localised damage not usually serious.

Treatment: good garden hygiene and soil cultivation will usually reduce the areas available for the weevils to hide. Dust or spray with gamma-HCH regularly on foliage, in soil and in potting compost.

Woodlice
Armadillium vulgare

Description: pest which like damp shady places and feed on organic plant debris. Feed at night causing damage to roots, stems and leaves especially in cucumbers, tomatoes and orchids.

Symptoms: grey, hard-coated pests visible.

Treatment: spray or dust with gamma-HCH, or pirimiphos-methyl, around the base of the plants and in hiding places. Remove garden debris.

DISEASES

AN ALPHABETICAL GLOSSARY

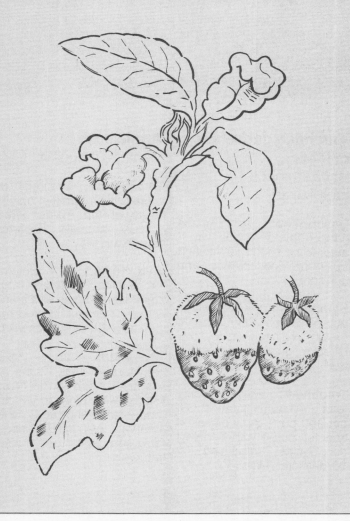

American gooseberry mildew
Sphaerotheca mors-uvae

Description: a disease caused by a fungus which attacks the shoots leaves and fruits of gooseberries and currants.

Symptoms: a white fungal powder which later turns light brown, and becomes felt-like. Checks growth and spoils fruit.

Treatment: regular pruning to improve air circulation. Cut out and burn badly diseased shoots. Spray with benomyl or benlate repeating at 10-day intervals.

Apple scab
Venturia inequalis

Description: a fungal disease which strikes only in trees of the malus genus. Occurs annually. Severest after a wet May.

Symptoms: sooty blotches on leaves, blistered twigs, dark scabs, spots and cracking on the fruit. Stored fruit can have black sunken spots.

Treatment: burn fallen leaves and twigs. Prune out diseased wood and burn also. Spray with dinocap at pink bud stage and at 2 week intervals. Also spray benomyl at green cluster and 2 week intervals.

Apple canker
Nectria galligena

Description: a common fungus disease which may also affect pears, beech, ash, poplar etc. It enters through the wounds caused by the likes of woolly aphids.

Symptoms: white pustules on the sunken bark. Small red bodies developing later.

Treatment: cut out and burn affected branches. Paint wound with white lead paint or canker paint. Spray with Bordeaux mixture after fruit is picked but before leaf-fall.

Black spot
Diplocarpon rosae

Description: a disease which attacks roses and can occur in mid-June — especially in heavily pruned roses like Hybrid teas.

Symptoms: blackish purple spots ¼-inch in diameter, first on lower leaves later higher up. Leaf turns yellow and falls early.

Treatment: disease overwinters in leaves so pick off and burn. Burn all debris at end of season. Spray every two weeks with captan or maneb. First spray immediately after pruning.

Brown rot
Sclerotinia species

Description: this is a fungal disease attacking most tree fruits and nuts including apples, apricots, cherries, pears, peach and plums. It occurs on injured fruit.

Symptoms: brown patches and rings of white fungal spores appearing on fruit in summer.

Treatment: throw away all damaged or withered fruit and prune off any dead shoots. Cut out and burn any canker. Spray fruit before picking in mid-August and early September with thiophanate-methyl to reduce rotting when storing.

Chlorosis

Description: a problem which leads to a loss of leaf colour. Can be caused by virus diseases or mineral deficiency and occurs more frequently in plants grown on chalky soil.

Symptoms: the green of the leaf is lost. Leaves turn pale-green yellow or sometimes white.

Treatment: chlorosis is usually due to a loss of acidity in the soil. Add peat and use an acid fertiliser. If it is caused by virus disease such treatment won't work. Remove and destroy affected plants.

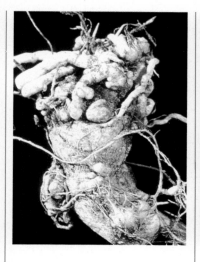

Club root
Plasmodiophora
brassicae

Description: a very serious fungal infection which attacks brassicas and turnips as well as wallflowers stocks and radishes. Prevalent in acid and badly-drained soils.

Symptoms: swollen and distorted roots, yellowing and ailing foliage.

Treatment: improve drainage, crop rotation and add hydrated lime at 14lbs per 30 sq. yards. Put 4% calomel dust into planting holes at 4 oz. per 20 plants or dip roots in benomyl solution (½ oz. to 1½ galls. water), to which wallpaper adhesive has been added. If severe sterilise with dazomet.

Damping off
Pythium species

Description: parasitic fungi attack seedlings causing them to collapse and die. Generally happens in the vegetable garden especially among young lettuces.

Symptoms: rotting and collapsing of plants at soil level.

Treatment: often the result of overcrowding or growing in wet conditions. Follow correct sowing procedure. Use clean pots and sterilised compost. Water seed boxes with Cheshunt compound, captan or zineb.

Downy mildew

Description: a disease caused by fungi and which attacks brassicas lettuce, onions and spinach. Spreads deep into plant tissue producing spores.

Symptoms: a furry coating underneath leaves. Yellow patches on the surface.

Treatment: good, regular cultivation of the plot. Spray brassicas, spinach and onions with zineb. Dust onions with Bordeaux powder. Treat lettuces with thiram.

Foot rot

Description: a problem arising most commonly in herbaceous plants, tomatoes, peas and beans. Caused by a variety of fungi.

Symptoms: a blackening and rotting at the base of stems which will usually lead to the death of the plant. Some fungi produce spores that overwinter in soil.

Treatment: if persistent, grow plants in sterilised soil. Rotate crops. Water young plants with captan or zineb.

Gall

Outgrowths which develop on the leaves, stems, crowns and roots of a variety of plants may be gall. There are two types:

Crown Gall
Agrobacterium tumefaciens

Description: a bacterial disease which is found on fruits, vegetables and other plants.

Symptoms: large outgrowths, either hard or soft, which develop on roots and give plants a stunted appearance.

Treatment: enters through wounds so avoid damage. Burn any diseased plants. Dip roots of new plants in copper fungicide.

Leafy Gall
Corynebacterium fascians

Description: a bacterial disease affecting a variety of plants. Enters through wounds and is soil-borne.

Symptoms: leafy gall produces aborted shoots and thick distorted leaves. It spreads by propagation of diseased stock and from infected garden tools.

Treatment: no chemical cure. Avoid diseased stock. Keep garden tools clean. Burn any diseased plants.

Grey Mould
Botrytis Cinerea

Description: one of the most troublesome of all fungal diseases it attacks all plants through wounds and dead or decaying tissue. Can spread through contact.

Symptoms: rotting fruit covered in a soft, grey mould.

Treatment: spray with benomyl, dichlofluanid or thiophanatemethyl when flowers open and repeat every two weeks. Can fumigate with tecnazene.

Honey Fungus
Armillariella mellea

Description: a soil-borne parasite which causes more damage in the garden than almost any other. It attacks all plants though is most commonly found on trees and shrubs.

Symptoms: honey-coloured mushrooms growing from dead wood, white spreading fungal growths, black threads on roots.

Treatment: destroy diseased plants. Sterilise soil with mixture of one pint formaldehyde to 6 galls. water. Apply at 5 galls. per sq. yard.

Mosaic

Description: mosaic is a term which is used to refer to the symptoms of a number of virus diseases affecting raspberries, marrows and other plants.

Symptoms: a yellow blotching of the leaves which may also become distorted. On green leaves it can show as pale green mottling.

Treatment: dig up and destroy diseased plants. When buying ensure you get plants that are disease-free.

Peach Leaf Curl
Taphrina deformans

Description: a fungal disease which attacks peaches, nectarines, almonds, apricots and other related prunus varieties.

Symptoms: leaves have red blisters later turning white and then brown. Will fall prematurely.

Treatment: pick off and burn diseased leaves. Spray with benomyl or Bordeaux mixture in January or February and again 2 weeks later. Spray again just before leaf fall (autumn).

Petal Blight
Itersonilia perplexans

Description: a serious disease affecting a number of plants including outdoor chrysanthemums and vegetables, especially globe artichokes.

Symptoms: brown spots on the petals, rotting flowers. Eventually petal tissue will die. Especially prevalent in chilly summers and in wet conditions.

Treatment: spray with zineb before the flowers open and repeat weekly. Destroy any diseased flowers.

Potato Blight
Phytopthora infestans

Description: the most serious of all potato diseases it can spread rapidly destroying whole crops. Also attacks tomatoes. Can develop any time between May and August. Prevalent in wet areas and in wet summers.

Symptoms: yellow-brown patches on leaves. White fungal threads under leaves in wet weather. Rotting tubers and haulms.

Treatment: Spray with zineb, maneb or Bordeaux mixture at two week intervals especially in a wet season. Start before tops meet in the rows.

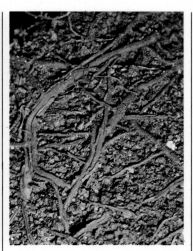

Powdery Mildew

Description: a general term which applies to a variety of fungi. Found in stems and leaves. Some attack specific plants others a whole range.

Symptoms: white, powdery coating on the leaves, stems, shoots, flowers and sometimes fruit. Overwinter on host plant.

Treatment: remove all diseased shoots and destroy in autumn. Spray every two weeks in spring and summer with benomyl or dinocap. Dust ornamental plants with sulphur. Thrives in dried out soil so water and mulch.

Root rot

Description: a problem which can attack almost any type of plant and usually results when soil is either too wet or too dry or when fungal diseases like black root rot strike.

Symptoms: discoloured foliage, early leaf-fall, shoots die-back, plants collapse.

Treatment: most likely to occur in poor cultivation conditions so improve these. Destroy infected plants. Rotate crops. Water with captan, Cheshunt compound or zineb.

Rust

Description: rust is a term confusingly applied to any sort of brown orange or red discoloration. It is, in fact, a fungal parasite which lives on plants.

Symptoms: brown, orange or yellow raised masses of spores on leaves or stems.

Treatment: cut out and burn diseased shoots in spring. Remove and burn dead stalks and debris in autumn. Best to destroy infested perennials. On vegetables and herbs it may indicate a Potassium deficiency. Under glass, spray with zineb every two weeks. On trees, shrubs or fruit may indicate malnutrition. Feed, mulch, water.

Silver Leaf
Stereum purpureum

Description: a fungal disease which commonly attacks many trees, especially plums. The Victoria is particularly prone. Air-borne spores enter through wounds.

Symptoms: silvery leaves turning brown when severe. Surfaces peel easily. Dieback and even death of branches. Infected branches have brown or purple stain showing when cut across and moistened.

Treatment: cut off infected branches to 6 ins. below the stain then paint with fungicidal paint. Water and feed regularly.

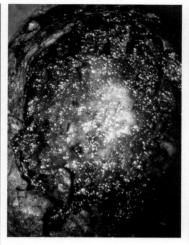 

Soft Rot
Erwinia carotovora

Description: a bacterial disease which attacks plant tissue reducing it to a soft mush which often smells revolting. Enters via wounds.

Symptoms: commonly attacks plants grown in badly drained soil. Can also attack bulbs and root vegetables stored in damp or moist conditions.

Treatment: destroy infected plants, bulbs and vegetables. Good garden hygiene and drainage. Cut out damaged tissue before bacteria enter.

Sooty Mould

Description: a black fungus resembling felt which grows on the honeydew secreted by aphids, scale insects, mealybugs and whiteflies. Reduces plant's access to light preventing food manufacture.

Symptoms: weakening of plants. Black fungal growth.

Treatment: attacking aphids should remove the main problem (see aphids). Otherwise painstaking removal of fungus with cloth soaked in water.

Tomato blight
Phytophthora infestans

Description: a serious disease affecting outdoor tomato plants which can kill off fruits if not controlled.

Symptoms: brown areas on the leaves, dark streaks on stems and reddish brown marbling on the green fruit which will later shrivel up and waste away. Particularly prevalent in wet summers.

Treatment: spray every two weeks with Bordeaux mixture, maneb or zineb — especially in wet weather.

Virus disease

Description: tiny organisms can enter plant tissue via wounds in outer skin causing a wide variety of plant problems. Most are spread by insects, especially aphids.

Symptoms: varied according to the plant. Commonly leaves and stems change colour. There is wilting, stunting and the development of outgrowths.

Treatment: no chemical treatment. Destroy affected plants. Stock with virus-free plants. Good garden hygiene. Control insects, especially aphids, which might bring virus diseases in.

OTHER DISEASES

Arabis mosaic virus

Description: a virus which attacks a wide range of plants – bulbous, herbaceous and woody – and which can cause quite serious damage to fruit crops like raspberries and strawberries. Also attacks vegetables like celery and horseradish.

Symptoms: shows itself in the very course variegation of leaves and in reduced plant growth. Yellow blotching on the leaves.

Treatment: buy stock that is certified virus-free. Affected plants should be dug up and destroyed.

Bacterial canker
Aplanobacter populi

Description: a bacterial disease spread by rain and transferred from one tree to another by insects. Bacteria enter through leaf or scars on bud-scale.

Symptoms: shows itself as a cream-coloured slime coming out of cracks in the wood of one-year-old shoots.

Treatment: no effective chemical control. Cut out any shoots that are badly infected. Paint wounds with protective paint. Destroy trees if severely affected.

Basal rot

Description: a disease which causes bulbs to rot and which especially attacks bulbs such as lilium.

Symptoms: disease begins at the base of the bulb spreading upwards and can destroy the whole bulb. May be affected by fungi such as Fusarium wilt but can also come from fungi and bacterium entering through wounds and dead tissue.

Treatment: if caught early cut out diseased roots and tissue and dip bulbs in benomyl solution. Dust with quintozene and rake fungicide into soil. Destroy diseased bulbs.

Bitter pit

Description: a common disorder affecting apples which will appear on half-grown fruit or on those in storage. Disease is more common in hot, dry summers and may be connected with water shortage at important times.

Symptoms: brown spots on the skin and throughout the flesh. No rotting.

Treatment: feed and mulch the tree with well-decomposed compost and water before soil dries out. In mid-June spray with calcium nitrate at 8 tablespoons to 5 gallons of water. Repeat at three week intervals.

Black leg

Description: a disease which can affect potatoes and also attacks cuttings of pelargoniums and outdoor plants. Most likely to occur in cold and wet soil and is caused by a number of fungi.

Symptoms: a characteristic black rot develops at the base of the stem. Leaves turn yellow and the stem softens and dies.

Treatment: remove and burn all seriously diseased plants. Prevent trouble by good gardening hygiene and strict greenhouse controls. Sterilised compost.

Blindness

Description: a problem affecting many bulbous plants like narcissi and tulips – especially those grown in containers.

Symptoms: flower failure. Plants tend to produce only leaves, and sometimes flower buds, which wither and turn brown.

Treatment: usually caused by excessive dryness in the roots or, paradoxically, water-logging. Prevent problem by making sure bulbs have satisfactory drainage system.

Bud-drop

Description: a problem which manifests itself, as its name suggests, by the dropping of buds before flowering. Afflicts many plants including runner beans. Usually due to poor cultural conditions.

Symptoms: buds or partly open flowers drop before pollination causing total crop failure.

Treatment: mulch heavily and water well during dry periods.

Blue mould
Penicillium species

Description: a disease which produces masses of fungal spores and is readily identifiable. Occurs in plant material in store. Found as a secondary fungus on injured or dying tissue.

Symptoms: distinctive masses of blue-green or green fungal spores.

Treatment: examine stored material regularly. Keep storage conditions dry and cool and ensure you only store healthy fruit. Dust bulbs, but not vegetables, with quintozene before storing.

Black Spot
Diplocarpon rosae

Description: this is a disease which generally affects roses but which can also occur on climbers like blackcurrant bushes. It is a disease which generally occurs on heavily pruned bushes and establishes itself in mid-June, though symptoms may show themselves as early as April or May. It is especially prevalent in Hybrid tea roses. The disease will overwinter on the leaves of bushes.

Symptoms: black spot shows itself as blackish/purple spots which are some $\frac{1}{4}$ inch in diameter. They show first on lower leaves gradually appearing higher up. Leaves turn yellow and tend to fall early.

Treatment: pick off and burn any infected leaves and burn garden debris to kill off any overwintering traces. Control the disease by spraying every two weeks with captan, dichlofluanid or maneb. Apply the first treatment immediately after pruning. The disease tends to gain hold on weak bushes so apply a foliar feed.

Blossom end rot

Description: shows itself as a rotting on the skin at the blossom end of tomatoes. It is usually caused by drought.

Symptoms: brown or black patches at the blossom end of the fruit which enlarge and can penetrate into the flesh. Caused by drought at the critical stage of young fruit development.

Treatment: don't let the soil dry out and this problem should not appear.

Cane spot
Elsinoe veneta

Description: a fungal disease common to raspberries especially in the north of England and Kent. Varieties 'Norfolk Giant'' and ''Lloyd George'' are susceptible. Also attacks other rosaceous plants.

Symptoms: purple spots turning into large white ones on the canes and leading to splitting. Spotted and distorted fruit.

Treatment: cut out and burn spotted canes. Spray remaining ones with benomyl at bud burst then every two weeks until blossoming ends.

Chocolate spot
Botrytis fabae

Description: a fungal disease which is usually not too serious. It affects broad beans and is common in humid weather.

Symptoms: dark-brown (chocolate) spots appear on the leaves and stems in June/July but may also appear in December/ January after frosts. Weak plants are more susceptible to attack.

Treatment: sow thinly and promote strong growth with potash and lime fertiliser. If serious spray with copper fungicide.

Coral spot
Nectria cinnabarina

Description: a fungus normally found living on dead wood but which can also enter living tissue and destroy entire bushes. Red currants are especially susceptible.

Symptoms: red cushions of spores massed on wood.

Treatment: cut diseased wood back to 6 ins. below affected area. Paint wound with sealing paint.

Cucumber mosaic virus

Description: one of the most troublesome of the whole range of virus diseases, it is caused by a wide range of hosts and is readily transmitted by aphids. Affects not only cucumbers but marrows and other related plants. Can be carried on gardening tools.

Symptoms: greenish-yellow mottling on the leaves and fruit. Stunted growth and puckered fruit.

Treatment: control aphids and other carriers by spraying. Destroy affected plants the moment they are detected.

Dry rot
Fusarium species

Description: a storage disease which is common in potatoes and usually develops from January onwards. Most troublesome in early-maturing varieties.

Symptoms: as the name suggests – a dry rotting in the tubers.

Treatment: the disease thrives in poor storage conditions and can develop rapidly in humid environment. Store only healthy tubers in cool, dry place. Destroy affected tubers.

Dutch elm disease
Ceratocystis ulmi

Description: a fungal disease which has laid waste vast numbers of noble trees throughout the English landscape. It is spread by elm bark beetles which lay their eggs in weakened or dying elm trees.

Symptoms: die-back of branch leaders followed by the rapid death of the trees.

Treatment: there is no successful treatment of the disease. Keeping a healthy tree resistant to the disease is the best way. Chop down and destroy badly infected trees.

Eye rot
Nectria galligena

Description: a fungal disease affecting apple and sometimes pear trees. Rot extends through the fruit until it is all affected. Caused by apple canker fungus.

Symptoms: the disease first occurs at the eye-end, thus its name. Diseased fruits have a characteristic flattened appearance at the eye end and fall early.

Treatment: control as for apple canker. Cut out and burn small branches and spurs. Use canker paint after pruning to avoid exposed cuts. Use DNC spray at bud break and mercury spray when dormant.

Fireblight
Erwinia amylovora

Description: a bacterial disease afflicting pears, apples and ornamental trees and shrubs of the Rosaceae family.

Symptoms: attacks growing trees through the flowers which turn black. Leaves brown and wither, shoots die back and canker develops at the base. Cankers remain dormant in the spring becoming active as blossoms open.

Treatment: Inform the Ministry of Agriculture. Fireblight is a notifiable disease. Treatment involves cutting all diseased wood out and back to a point up to 4 ft. below the infected areas.

Grey bulb rot
Rhizoctonia tuliparum

Description: a fungal disease most commonly affecting tulips and hyacinths but which can also strike in a range of other plants especially forced crocus fritillaria, gladiolus, iris and narcissus.

Symptoms: black fungus develops in rotting tissue and contaminates the soil affecting nearby plants.

Treatment: remove and destroy all effected plants and surrounding soil. Burn plant debris from diseased plants. Dip bulbs in benomyl solution then dust with quintozene and rake quintozene into soil before planting.

Magnesium deficiency

Description: Magnesium is one of the important constituents of chlorophyl and its absence shows itself in discoloration of the foliage. It is likely to be deficient in light, acid soils. Particularly affects apples and tomatoes.

Symptoms: yellow bands between veins and brilliant orange/brown and red tints may develop.

Treatment: spray with magnesium sulphate – 8 tablespoons to 2½ gallons of water.

Mint rust
Puccinia menthae

Description: a fungus which attacks the Mentha species and can be very destructive in forced plants under glass. First appears in the spring.

Symptoms: thickened, distorted shoots and a spring fungus bearing orange spores. In summer spores are yellow while overwintering spores are black and form on the leaves towards the end of the season. They germinate the following spring producing spores which affect the rhizomes and stems.

Treatment: use only disease-free plants. Wash cuttings in water at a temp. of 41–46C for 10 minutes. Plunge in cold water before planting out.

Oedema

Description: a common problem occurring in the foliage of many plants and frequently affecting the ivy-leaved pelargoniums, camellia, succulent and semi-succulent plants. It is due to excessive moisture in the soil and/or atmosphere.

Symptoms: infected leaves have swollen tissue due to build up of water.

Treatment: improve atmosphere, and soil conditions, and plants will usually recover. Ventilate greenhouse. Keep plants just moist. Can occur as a reaction to chemical sprays.

Potassium deficiency

Description: lack of potassium causes stunted growth. It is one of the major plant requirements. Often it is deficient in light, peaty or chalky soils.

Symptoms: leaves turn bluish-green, browning at the tips and at leaf margins.

Leaves of broad-leaved plants curl downwards.

Treatment: remedy by the application of potassium fertilisers.

Rust

Description: rust is a term which is often confusingly applied to any sort of brown, orange or yellow discoloration. It is, however, a fungal parasite and should not be confused with anything else. In vegetables and herbs rust is most troublesome when they suffer a Potassium Deficiency. Under glass it builds up on carnations and chrysanthemums when it is too humid. With annuals and perennials it occurs most frequently when plants are grown under adverse conditions. And with trees and shrubs it occurs when soil conditions are too dry.

Symptoms: raised masses of brown, orange or yellow spores on leaves or stems.

Treatment: cut out and burn any diseased shoots in the spring. Dead stalks and garden debris should be removed and burned in the autumn. With vegetables controls are not usually necessary. On plants under glass increase ventilation and spray at 10-day intervals with maneb or thiram. Annuals and perennials should be sprayed with maneb or thiram at two week intervals. With trees and shrubs mulch and water, and spray small shrubs with thiram or zineb at two week intervals.

Scab

Description: a fungal disease on fruit and vegetables particularly inclined to attack apples and pears.

Symptoms: olive-green blotches on the leaves. Early leaf-fall, scabs on fruit (brown-black), cracking skins.

Treatment: spray regularly from first flower buds until July with benomyl, captan or thiram. Burn diseased leaves.

Shothole

Description: holes in the leaves, particularly on cherries, nectarines, peaches, plums and ornamental prunus varieties. Also spinach and horse-radish. Can be caused either by bacterial or fungal diseases.

Symptoms: brown patches on the leaves turning into holes caused by the falling away of dead tissue.

Treatment: feed and water properly. Spray if problem persists in summer, with half-strength copper fungicide. Also spray in autumn with full-strength copper fungicide as leaves fall.

Wire stem
Rhizoctonia solani

Description: a disease affecting a variety of young plants particularly cauliflowers and other brassicas.

Symptoms: in young seedlings it can cause damping-off (see page   ) and later it shows as browning and shrinking of stem bases which can cause the stunting or even the death of the plant.

Treatment: use sterilised compost to raise seedlings or rake quintozene into soil before sowing outdoors.

WEEDS

AN ALPHABETICAL GLOSSARY

Chickweed
Stellaria media

Description: a low-growing annual weed which enjoys moist soil and which will flower and farm seeds even in winter.

Symptoms: will grow anywhere and can be highly invasive. Fine roots pale green soft oval leaves.

Treatment: regular weeding and hoeing.

Couch grass
Agrophyron repens

Description: officially a herb it spreads rapidly by sections of its rhizomes forming deep underground runners which intertwine with roots of garden plants especially fruit bushes.

Symptoms: recognised by tall whispy shoots with thin clusters of seed heads.

Treatment: Dalapon under fruit bushes — paraquat/diquat between vegetables. Forks up easily in a vegetable plot.

Creeping buttercup
Ranunculus repens

Description: a perennial weed which has an erect, hairy much-branched form with long stalked leaves divided into segments. Flowers are yellow and borne on grooved stalks.

Symptoms: it spreads strongly by extensive underground runners and tends to be most troublesome on poorly drained soil.

Treatment: regular weeding. Spot treatment with 2,4-D or with paraquat/diquat.

Creeping thistle
Cirsium arvense

Description: perennial weed growing up to three feet in height.

Symptoms: reproduces rapidly by means of rhizomes which spread some distance from the parent plant. It also reproduces by seed from the bulbous, tufted seed pods carried at the top of the weed.

Treatment: control under fruit bushes with dichlobenil or spot treat with 2,4-D. In between vegetables treat with paraquat/diquat.

Daisies
Bellis perennis

Description: a lawn weed which has given rise to a number of far more accept-able garden varieties. Grows to 4 ins. Flowers have a white, ray-like floret encircling a yellow disc. Blooms March to October.

Symptoms: clumps of the plant growing at the expense of grasses or other plants.

Treatment: apply 2,4-D, fenoprop or 2,4-D weed-killers.

Dandelion
Taraxacum officinale

Description: a perennial herb with deep tap-roots, leaves and stems which produce a milky sap when cut. Yellow flower-heads 6 cms. across flowering April to October.

Symptoms: reproduces from seed and from sections of its fleshy tap-roots.

Treatment: it is quite easy to pull up in a vegetable plot but in lawns and under fruit bushes and trees spot treat with 2,4-D or mecoprop.

Fat hen
Chenopodium album

Description: Probably the first plant ever harvested by man but now considered a weed. Erect with a sometimes red stem and small greenish white clusters of flowers.

Symptoms: springs up on waste ground and tends to colonise areas fairly rapidly.

Treatment: an annual, it should be kept under control by regular weeding.

Red Dead Nettle
Labiatae maculatum

Description: invasive and difficult to eliminate from most soils, especially sticky ones, this nettle grows to 12 ins. and will grow easily in poor soil.

Symptoms: mid-green leaves with a silver stripe down the centre. Flowers 1 inch long in May can be anything from pink to purple.

Treatment: dig out making sure all of the rhizome is removed. Control with repeated doses of 2,4-D or mecoprop.

Nettles
Urtica dioica (common nettle)

Description: a variety of weeds which can be highly invasive in the garden.

Symptoms: nettles reproduce by means of strong underground runners, spreading very rapidly and also growing to great height.

Treatment: among vegetables weed by hand (gloved) while among fruit trees and bushes control with repeated doses of 2,4-D and 2,4.5-T or mecoprop. If waste land on which no crop will be grown use the more potent sodium chlorate but be very careful.

Plantain (ribwort)
Plantago lanceolata

Description: a perennial with long leaves which thrives in poor soil and in lawns. Classed by many as a herb and not a weed but can be invasive and resistant to control.

Symptoms: long narrow leaves growing to 6 ins. and with parallel veins. Brownish flowers carried on four petals and in spikes.

Treatment: a single application of 2,4-D or Fenoprop +2,4-D. Remove individual plants by hand.

Plantain
Plantago major

Description: distinguished from the ribwort plantain by its longer flower head and thicker leaves this is also a perennial herb to some and a weed to others.

Symptoms: leaves grown to 6 ins. long and almost as wide. The whole plant will grow to some 9 ins. with a flower stalk that can be as long as 6 ins. Brownish flowers.

Treatment: a single application of 2,4-D or Fenoprop +2,4-D. Remove individual plants by hand.

Shepherd's Purse
Capsella bursa-pastoris

Description: an erect annual or biennial herb which is either hairless or has unbranched hairs. Deeply lobed leaves with small white flowers all year round. Triangular fruit pods.

Symptoms: appears on waste ground. Grows up to 15 ins. and reproduces strongly by seed.

Treatment: regular cultivation.

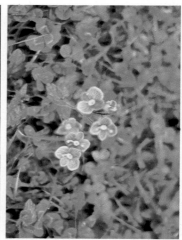

Sow thistle
Sonchus oleraceus (no
   spines)
Sonchus asper (spines)

Description: two species,
one with and one without
spines. Both can grow to 30
ins. in good soil.

Symptoms: an annual weed
which can become invasive if
allowed to spread.

Treatment: like most annuals
it can be satisfactorily controlled by regular weeding in
the garden.

Speedwell
Veronica

Description: a creeping
perennial herb which has four
tiny white or pale blue flowers
with terminal spikes.
Commonly found in grass-
land or heathland.

Symptoms: unless con-
trolled in the garden speed-
well can form a dense mat.
Reproduces strongly by
seed.

Treatment: regular weeding
and hoeing should keep it
away. Dig out roots and burn.
Don't use for compost.

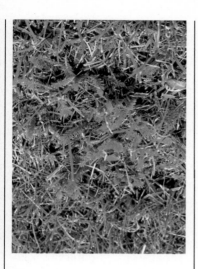

Yarrow
Achillea millefolium

Description: a creeping aromatic perennial herb with erect, woolly stems and dark-green leaves. White or pink flowerheads in dense, terminal clusters.

Symptoms: can be a lawn weed, spreading through its roots which are inclined to spread out throwing up fresh shoots.

Treatment: two or three applications of CMPP or 2,4-D at intervals of 21 days in early summer. Scarify the lawn as a follow-up treatment.

OTHER WEEDS

Ground elder
Aegopodium podagraria

Description: A low-growing weed which is a menace in the cultivated garden. A rampant-spreader it reproduces by sections of rhizomes.

Symptoms: clusters of white flowers in May to July. Grows to 2 ft.

Treatment: repeated applications of dichlobenil, 2,4-D, 2,4,5-T or diquat/paraquat.

Horsetail
Equisetum arvense

Description: a creeping perennial weed which reproduces by its spores and rhizomes.

Symptoms: aerial stems first pale brown without branches and later green and sterile. Spores ripen in April in ovoid terminal cones.

Treatment: repeated applications of dichlobenil or spot treatments of 2,4-D.

Creeping yellow cress
Rorippa sylvestris

Description: a creeping yellow, hairless perennial weed which is especially troublesome in badly-drained soil. Reproduces by stems and seeds.

Symptoms: grows to two feet with four yellow petals twice as long as its sepals in June to August.

Treatment: control with repeated applications of dichlobenil. On vegetable plots use paraquat/diquat.

Large bindweed
Calystegia sepium

Description: a large climbing plant which is difficult to control merely by repeated digging. Creeps above and below ground and if roots are chopped each piece grows into a separate plant.

Symptoms: pink, bell-like flowers which shut tightly when it rains. Roots, which look like a mass of spaghetti, penetrate many feet below ground.

Treatment: control with repeated applications of dichlobenil or spot-treatments of 2,4-D. In vegetable plots use paraquat/diquat.

Dock
Rumex species

Description: there are two main problem docks in the garden – the broad-leaved dock (Rumex obtusifolius) and the curled dock (Rumex crispus). Both reproduce by seeds and rootstock.

Symptoms: as their name suggests they are distinguished by their leaves – one with broad, sturdy leaves the other with narrow curling ones. Both are difficult to eradicate and will reproduce from the smallest piece of root if left in the soil.

Treatment: repeated applications of dichlobenil or spot-treatments of 2,4-D or mecoprop. Dig out by hand trying to remove all the roots.

Colt's foot
Tussilago farfara

Description: while a genuine herb as opposed to a weed – it has many uses including as an infusion against catarrh – it can become a nuisance in the garden unless controlled. A creeping perennial it likes waste places especially in clay soil.

Symptoms: long white scaly prostrate stems, yellow flowers in March to April.

Treatment: Dig out removing all the roots. Repeated applications of dichlobenil or paraquat/diquat in the vegetable plot.

Plantain
Plantago species

Description: a family of plants which seem to thrive in lawns. Includes the Greater Rat's Tail, Hoary or Lamb's Tongue and Ribwort. Once prized for its ability to cure bruises, cuts and wounds.

Symptoms: attractive plant with rosettes of daisy-like leaves and spikey flowers, given a furry appearance by their purple or yellow stamens. Tough, wiry stems.

Treatment: a single application of 2,4-D or Fenoprop + 2,4-D. Remove individual plants by hand.

Field Woodrush
Lazula campestris

Description: a strong, invasive weed fond of lawns and

which needs determined work to remove all traces.

Symptoms: grows to one foot. Leaves have long, sparse, white hairs. Small brown flowers with transparent margins.

Treatment: two or three applications of fenoprop + 2,4-D at three weekly intervals. Scarify the lawn to weaken any remaining plants.

Index Code

1. Destroy affected parts.	24. Dinocap.
2. Do not overcrowd.	25. HCH.
3. Sterilise compost or soil.	26. Burn leaves and twigs.
4. Benomyl.	27. Cut out canker.
5. Captan.	28. Destroy mummified fruits.
6. Thiram.	29. Hand pick insects.
7. Zineb.	30. Rotate crops.
8. Derris.	31. Dressed seed.
9. Dimethoate.	32. Poison bait.
10. Malathion.	33. Clean containers and tools.
11. Pyrethrum.	34. Banding grease.
12. Trichlorphon.	35. Dichlofluanid.
13. Gamma-HCH.	36. Lime sulphur.
14. Diazinon.	37. Lime seedbed to give Ph of 7.
15. Basamid	38. Calomel dust in planting holes.
16. Copper fungicide.	39. Avoid over-watering.
17. Bromophos	40. Dicofol.
18. Winter wash.	41. Bordeaux mixture.
19. Tar oil.	42. Avoid excessive damp.
20. DNC Spray.	
21. Canker paint.	
22. Fenitrothion.	
23. Prune out shoots.	

The pictorial glossary, pages 23–82, will have helped you to identify your problem. Here is a list of the more common pests and diseases which affect particular varieties, with code numbers alongside each. The numbers refer to an index of treatments on page 83 which will tell you how to control your problem.

African Violet

Crown rot. **1, 2, 3.**
Grey Mould. **1, 2, 4, 5, 6.**

Alyssum

Downy Mildew. Spray **6, 7.**

Anemone

Aphids. Spray **8, 9, 10.**
Caterpillars. **8, 11, 12.**
Downy Mildew. Spray **6, 7.**
Rust. Spray **7.**

Antirrhinum

Aphids. Spray **10.**
Cutworms. Treat soil with **13.**
Downy Mildew. Spray **6, 7.**
Eelworms. **1.**
Foot rot. **3.**
Leaf spot. **1.** Sterilise soil with **15.**
Rust. Spray **6, 7.**

Shot hole. Spray 16.
Wilt. **3.** Water soil with **4.**

Apple

Aphids. **18, 19, 8.**
Apple Canker. **20, 21.**
Apple Capsid. Spray **9, 22.**
Apple Mildew. **23.** Spray **24.**
Apple Sawfly. **25.**
Apple Scab. **26** and spray **4.**
Brown Rot. **27, 28.**
Codling Moth. Spray **10, 22.**
Tortrix Moth. Spray **22.**
Leaf Hoppers. Spray **9, 10.**

Asparagus

Asparagus Beetle. **29,** Spray **8, 13.**
Asparagus Rust. **1.** Spray **6, 7.**

Beans Broad

Aphids. Spray **8, 10.**

Bean Weevils. Spray **13, 22.**
Chocolate Spot. Spray **6, 4.**
Damping Off. Spray **6, 30.**

Beans Dwarf French

Aphids. Spray **9, 10, 13.**
Foot Rot. **1, 3.**
Red Spider Mite. Spray **9, 10.**

Beans Runner

Aphids. Spray **8, 10.**
Botrytis. Spray **4.**
Foot Rot. **30, 31.**
Red Spider Mite. Spray **8, 9.**
Slugs. **32.**

Beetroot

Blackfly. Spray **10.**
Downy Mildew. Spray **6, 7, 16.**
Leaf Spot. **1, 16.**
Slugs. **32.**
Mosaic Virus. Spray **10.**

Begonia

Bacterial Blight. **1, 33.**
Powdery Mildew. Spray **6.**
Root Rot. **3, 33.**
Thrips. **13.**

Vine Weevil. **34, 13** in compost.
Virus. Spray **10.**
Whitefly. Spray **6.**

Blackberry

Aphids. Spray **8, 9, 10.**
Blackberry Mite. **1.**
Botrytis/Grey Mould. Spray **4, 35.**
Cane Blight. **1.**
Cane Spot. Spray **4, 6, 35.**
Leaf Hoppers. Spray **9, 10.**

Blackcurrant

American Gooseberry Mildew.
Spray **4, 24.**
Aphids. Spray **8, 9, 10.**
Big Bud. Spray **36.**
Blackcurrant Sawfly. Spray **8, 10, 22.**
Capsid. Spray **9, 22, 13.**
Caterpillars. **29.** Spray **9.**
Eelworm. **1.**
Red Spider Mite. **18.**
Leaf Spot. Spray **4, 24.**
Mildew. Spray **4, 24.**
Rust. Spray **7.**
Tortrix Moths. Spray **22.**

Brassicas.
Brussels sprouts, broccoli, cabbage, cauliflowers, radish, swede, turnip etc.

Aphids. Spray **9, 10.**
Cabbage Moth. Spray or dust **8, 22, 12.**
Cabbage Root Fly. **25, 14, 9, 12.**
Cabbage White Butterfly. Spray or dust **8, 12, 22.**
Cabbage Whitefly. **1.** Spray **9, 10.**
Canker. Soak seeds in **6.**
Club Root. **30, 3, 37, 38.**
Damping Off. **3.** Water seeds in **6.**
Downy Mildew. Spray **6, 7.**
Grey Mould. **4, 35** on seedlings.
Mildew. **4, 24.**
Mosaic Virus. **1.**
Turnip Fly. Spray **8.**

Camellia

Leaf Blotch. **1.**
Mealybugs. Spray **13, 14.**
Scale Insects. Spray **10, 14.**

Carnation

Aphids. Spray **9, 10.**

Carnation Fly. Spray or dust **13.**
Carnation Spider Mite. Spray **9, 10.**
Caterpillars. **29.** Spray **9.**
Grey Mould. Spray **4, 35.**
Leaf Spot. Spray **6, 7.**
Powdery Mildew **4, 24.**
Ring Spot. Spray **7.**
Rust. **1.** Spray **6, 7.**
Stem Rot. **3, 39.** Drench cuttings in **5.**
Virus. **1.** Spray **9, 10.**

Carrot

Aphids. Spray **9, 10.**
Black Rot. **1.**
Botrytis. **4.**
Carrot Fly. Dust with **5, 6, 13** or **25.**
Eelworm. **30.**
Soft Rot. **1, 30.**

Celery

Aphids. Spray **9, 10.**
Carrot Fly. Dust with **5, 6, 13.**
Celery Fly. Spray **10.**
Leaf Miner. (as for Celery Fly)
Virus. (as Aphids)

Cherry

Aphids. Spray **9, 10.**

Bacterial Canker. Spray **16.**
Brown Rot. **18.**
Caterpillars. **19, 29.**
Red Spider Mite. **18.**
Leaf Hoppers. Spray **9, 10.**
Plum Fruit Moth. **19.**
Plum Sawfly. Spray **9, 22.**
Plum Tortrix Moth. Spray **22.**
Scale Insects. Spray **10, 19.**
Thrips. Spray **9.**
Winter Moth. Spray **22, 19.**

Chrysanthemum

Aphids. Spray **9, 10.**
Caterpillars. **19, 29.**
Leaf Miner. Spray **14, 13.**
Earwig. Spray **13.**
Red Spider Mite. **9.**
White Fly. **10, 14.**
Grey Mould. **1, 33.** Spray
    stems with **5.**
Eelworm. **30.**
Petal Blight. Spray **7.**
Powdery Mildew. Spray **4, 24.**
Root Rot. Drench soil with **5,
    7.**
Rust. Spray **6, 7.**
Stem Rot. **3.**

Cucumber

Aphids. Spray **9, 10.**
Black Root Rot. **1, 3.**
Red Spider Mite. **18.**

Whitefly. Smokes of **25.**
    Spray **13.**
Grey Mould. **1.** Spray **4.**
Millipedes. **3.** Drench soil with
    13.
Powdery Mildew. Spray **4, 24.**
Stem/Root Rot. **3. 16** to base
    of plants.
Virus. **1, 33.**

Cyclamen

Aphids. **10.**
Black Root Rot. **1, 3, 33.**
    Water with **4, 5.**
Cyclamen Mite. Spray **40.**
Grey Mould. Spray **4.**
Vine Weevil. **34, 13** in potting
    compost.

Daffodil

Aphids. Spray **8, 9, 10.**
Basal Rot. **1.**
Bulb Mite. **1.**
Eelworm. **1.**
Narcissus Flies. **1.**
Smoulder. **1.** Spray **7.**

Dahlia

Aphids. Spray **8, 10, 25.**
Capsid Bug. Spray **9, 13.**
Caterpillars. Spray **8, 29.**

Red Spider Mite. Spray **9**.
Grey Mould. **2**. Spray **4**.
Leaf Gall. **1**.
Thrips. Spray **8, 10, 25**.
Virus. **1**. Spray **8, 10, 25**.

Delphinium

Black Blotch. Spray **41**.
Cutworms. **32**.
Delphinium Moth. **1**. Spray **25**.
Mildew. Spray **16**.
Slugs. **32**.

Forsythia

Dieback. **1**.
Galls. **1**.
Leaf Spot. Spray with **16**.

Freesia

Aphids. **8** or **10** as soil drench.
Core Rot. **1, 3**.
Dry Rot. **1, 3**.
Thrips. Spray **10**.

Fuschia

Grey Mould. **1, 2**. Spray with **4** or **35**.
Rust. Spray **16**.
Whitefly. Spray **10, 14**.

Gladiolus

as Freesia.

Gooseberry

Gooseberry Mildew. Spray **4, 24**.
Aphids. **19**.
Botrytis. Spray **4, 24**.
Capsid. Spray **9, 13, 22**.
Gooseberry Sawfly. Spray **8, 10, 22**.
Grey Mould. Spray **4, 24**.
Leaf Spot. Spray **4, 24**.
Rust. Spray **7**.

Honeysuckle

Leaf Spot. Spray **16**.
Mildew. Spray **16**.
Rust. Spray **16**.

Hyacinth

Black Slime. **1, 3**.
Grey Bulb Rot. **1, 3**.
Yellow Disease. **1, 3**.

Hydrangea

Aphids. Spray **8, 9, 10**.
Botrytis. **1, 2**. Spray **4, 5, 6**.

Capsid Bug. Spray **9, 22.**
Damping Off. **3, 33.** Water
 with **6.**
Grey Mould. **1, 2.** Spray **4, 5,
6.**
Mildew/Powdery Mildew.
 Spray **16.**
Whitefly. Smokes of **25.**
 Spray with   **10, 13.**

Iris

Aphids. Spray **8, 9, 10.**
Iris Sawfly. Dust with **25.**
Leaf Spot. **1.** Spray with **41.**
Mites. Spray **9.**
Rotting. **4.**
Rust. Spray **6, 7.**
Virus. **1.** Spray **8, 9, 10.**

Ivy

Leaf Spot. **1.** Spray **4.**
Scorching. **1.**
Whitefly. Spray **13, 10.**

Lavender

Aphids. Spray **8, 9, 10.**
Cuckoo Spit Bugs. Spray **10,
 13.**

Leek

Foot Rot. **3, 30.**

Leek Moth. **8, 22.**
Onion Fly. **38.** Spray **12.**
Rust. Spray **16.**

Lettuce

Aphids. Spray **9, 10.**
Black Root Rot. **1.**
Collar Rot. **3.**
Cutworms. **32.**
Damping Off. Water with **6,
 16.**
Downy Mildew. **1.** Spray **6, 7.**
Grey Mould. **1.** Spray **4.**
Leaf Spot. **4.**
Slugs and Snails. **32, 29.**
Virus. **3.**

Lilac

Bacterial Blight. **1.**
Silver Leaf. **1, 23.** Paint with
 19.
Lilac Wilt. **1, 3.**

Lily

Aphids. Dust with **13.**
Leaf Blight. Spray **4, 16.**
Leaf Spot. Spray **16.**
Lily Thrips. Dust **13.**
Root Rot. **42.**
Rust. **1.** Spray **16.**
Virus. **1.** Spray **8, 9, 10.**

Lupin

Brown Spot. Dust **16**.
Colour Change. **1**.

Marigold

Leaf Spot. Spray **16**.
Mildew. Spray **24**.

Marrow/Courgette

Aphids. Spray **8, 9, 10**.
Glasshouse Millipede.
   Drench soil with **13**.
Grey Mould. **1**. Spray **4**.
Powdery Mildew. Spray **24**.
Slugs and Snails. **32**.
Virus. **1, 3, 33**.

Mint

Cuckoo Spit Bugs. Spray **13**.
Eelworm. **1**.
Rust. **1**.

Onion

Botrytis Spray **4**.
Downy Mildew. Spray **7** or **41**.
Eelworm. **1, 30**.
Neck Rot. **31**.
Onion Fly. **31, 38**.

White Rot. **3, 30**.
Virus. **1, 3, 33**.

Orchids

Aphids. Spray **8, 9, 10**.
Citrus Mealy Bugs. Spray **13,
   14**.
Leaf and Heart Rot. Spray **16**.
Leaf Spot. Spray **16**.
Scale Insects. Spray **9, 10,
   14**.
Virus. **1**.

Paeony

Blight. Dust with **16**. Spray **4**.
Leaf Spot. Spray **16**.

Parsnip

Bacterial Soft Rot. **1.30**.
Carrot Fly. Dust **5, 6, 25**.
Sclerotina Rot. **1, 30**.
Soft Rot. **1, 30**.

Pea

Aphids. Spray **9, 10, 22**.
Black Root Rot. **30, 31**.
Damping Off. **31**.
Downy Mildew. **1, 7**.
Eelworm. **3, 30**.

Foot Rot. **3, 30, 31.**
Leaf Spot. **30, 31.**
Mildew/Powdery Mildew.
   Spray **24.**
Virus/Mosaic. **1, 3, 33.**
Pea Weevil. Spray **13, 22.**
Pea Midge. Spray **9, 22.**
Pea Moth. Spray **22.**
Pea Thrips. Spray **9, 22.**
Root Rot. **31.**

Peach

Aphids. Spray **8, 10.**
Blossom Wilt. **1, 23, 28.** Spray **4.**
Brown Rot. **1, 23, 28.** Spray **4.**
Brown Scale. Spray **10, 14, 19.**
Eelworm. **1, 3.**
Red Spider Mite. Spray **9, 10.**
Leaf Curl. **1.** Spray **16.**
Powdery Mildew. Spray **24.**

Pear

Aphids. Spray **8, 9, 10.**
Blossom Wilt. **1, 28.** Spray **4, 19.**
Capsid. Spray **9, 22.**
Caterpillars. Spray **13.**
Red Spider Mite. Spray **9.**
Pear Leaf Midge. Spray **10, 22.**
Pear Sawfly. Spray **13.**
Pear Scab. **1, 23.** Spray **4. 41.**

Pelargonium

Aphids. Spray **8, 9, 10.**
Black Root Rot. Water soil
   with **4.**
Caterpillars. **8** dust.
White Fly. Spray **4.**
Leaf Curl. **1.**
Rust. **1.** Spray **6, 7.**
Virus. **1.**

Pepper/Capsicum

Caterpillars. **29.** Spray **13.**
Grey Mould. Spray **4.**

Petunia

Aphids. Spray **8, 9, 10.**
Foot Rot. **3, 30, 31.**
Leaf Spot. **1.** Spray **16.**
Virus. **1.**

Phlox

Caterpillars. Spray **12.**
Eelworm. **1, 3.**
Leaf Spot. **1.** Spray **16.**
Powdery Mildew. Spray **24.**

Plum

Aphids. Spray **9, 10.**

Canker. Spray **41, 16.**
Blossom Wilt. **18, 19.**
Brown Rot. **18.**
Caterpillars. **18, 19.**
Red Spider Mite. **18, 9, 10.**
Leafhoppers. Spray **9, 10.**
Plum Sawfly. Spray **9, 22**
Scale Insects. Spray **19.**
Thrips. Spray **9.**
Winter Moth. Spray **22.**

Potato

Aphids. Spray **9, 10.**
Blight. **1, 7.**
Capsid Bugs. Spray
9, 22.
Cutworm. **32.**
Eelworm. **30, 15.**
Flea Beetles. Spray **8.**
Slugs. **32.**
Virus. Control aphids. **30.**

Primula

Aphids. Drench soil in **14.**
Cutworms. **32.**
Downy Mildew. **1.**
Whitefly. Spray **4.**
Grey Mould. Spray **4.**
Leaf Spot. **1.**
Slugs. **32.**
Virus. **1.**

Raspberry — See Blackberry

Rhododendron

Azalea Leaf Miner. Spray **13.**
Gall. **1.** Spray **41.**
Glasshouse Thrips. **13** or **10**
    smokes.
Glasshouse Whitefly. Spray
    10, 14.
Grey Mould. Spray **4.**
Leafhopper. Spray **9, 13, 10.**
Leaf Scorch. Spray **16.**
Rhododendron Bug. Spray
    10, 13.
Vine Weevil. **13** dust in soil.

Rhubarb

Crown Rot. **1.**
Honey Fungus. **1, 3.**
Leaf Spot. **1.** Spray **5, 7.**
Stem and Bulb Eelworms. **1,**
    30.
Caterpillars. Spray **22.**

Rose

Aphids. Spray **9, 10.**
Blackspot/Leafspot. **1.** Spray
    5, 7.
Capsid Bugs. Spray **10, 14.**
Caterpillars. Spray **8, 10.**
Downy Mildew. **1.** Spray **7.**

Grey Mould. **2.** Spray **4.**
Leafhopper. Spray **8, 10.**
Rust. **1.** Spray **6, 7.**
Sawfly. Spray **8, 13.**
Scale. Spray **10, 14.**
Thrips. Spray **8, 13.**
Virus. **1.**

Spinach

Aphids. Spray **8.**
Downy Mildew. Spray **7.**
Leaf Miner. Spray **12.**
Leaf Spot. Spray **16.**

Strawberry

Aphids. Spray **9, 10.**
Botrytis/Grey Mould. **4, 5, 6, 42.**
Capsid. Spray **9.**
Cuckoo Spit Bug. Spray **10.**
Cutworms. **32.**
Eelworm. **3.**
Red Spider Mite. Spray **9, 10.**
Leatherjackets. **32.**
Mildew. Spray **4, 24.**
Strawberry Tortrix Moth. Spray **8.**
Virus. **1, 3, 15.**

Sweet Pea

Downy Mildew. **1, 7.**

Foot Rot. **30, 31.**
Virus. Spray **9, 10.**
White Mould. Spray **4, 7.**

Tomato

Aphids. Spray **9, 10, 13.**
Canker. Spray **16, 3.**
Blight. Spray **7.**
Brown Rot. **3.**
Caterpillars. **29.** Spray **12.**
Damping Off. Soil drench in **7.**
Spider Mite. Spray **9, 10.**
Glasshouse Whitefly. Spray **10, 14.**
Grey Mould/Stem Rot. **1, 3, 33.** Spray **5** on stem bases.
Leaf Miner. Spray **9, 10, 14.**
Tomato Moth. **29.** Spray **12.**

Tulip

Aphids. Dust **13.**
Bulb Mite. **1.**
Eelworm. **1.**
Grey Bulb Rot. **1, 3.**
Shanking. **3, 33.**
Slugs. **32.**
Virus. **1.** Dust **13.**

Turnips. See Brassicas.

Viola

Aphids. Spray **8**.
Cutworms. **32**.
Foot Rot. **3**.
Rust. Spray **7**.
Virus. Spray **8**.

Wallflower

Black Mould. Spray **16**.

Club Root. **3, 30, 37, 38**.
Damping Off. **3**. Water seeds in **6**.
Downy Mildew. Spray **6, 7**.
Virus. **1**.

Zinnia

Grey Mould/Botrytis. **1, 2**.
Seedling Blight. **31**. Spray **7, 16**.

Production: Mercurius (UK) Ltd., 11 East Stockwell Street, Colchester, Essex.

Compilation: Trevor J. Wright.

Author: Tony Loynes.

Photography: Harry Smith Photographic Collection, Brian Tree, A-Z.

Layout: David Lester.

Phototypesetting: S. M. Studios, Colchester.

Printing: BV Kunstdrukkerij Mercurius-Wormerveer, Holland.

This edition published by Sphere Books Ltd., London, 1984.
Copyright: Mercurius (UK) Ltd.

IDENTIFICATION AND TREATMENT RECORD

Keeping an identification and treatment record will help you to keep a check on the effectiveness of the controls you use. Pests and diseases can build up immunity to chemicals and changing those you use will help to combat this.

PLANT VARIETY _____

WHEN PLANTED _____

PREVENTITIVE TREATMENT & TYPE _____

_____

WHEN APPLIED _____

_____

PEST/DISEASE IDENTIFIED: DATE _____

TREATMENT (CHEMICAL OR OTHER) _____

DATES TREATED _____

_____

COMMENTS_____

_____

PLANT VARIETY _____

WHEN PLANTED _____

PREVENTITIVE TREATMENT & TYPE _____

_____

WHEN APPLIED _____

_____

PEST/DISEASE IDENTIFIED: DATE _____

TREATMENT (CHEMICAL OR OTHER) _____

DATES TREATED _____

_____

COMMENTS_____

_____

PLANT VARIETY _____

WHEN PLANTED _____

PREVENTITIVE TREATMENT & TYPE _____

_____

WHEN APPLIED _____

_____

PEST/DISEASE IDENTIFIED: DATE _____

TREATMENT (CHEMICAL OR OTHER) _____

DATES TREATED _____

_____

COMMENTS_____

_____

_____

PLANT VARIETY _____

WHEN PLANTED _____

PREVENTITIVE TREATMENT & TYPE _____

_____

WHEN APPLIED _____

_____

PEST/DISEASE IDENTIFIED: DATE _____

TREATMENT (CHEMICAL OR OTHER) _____

DATES TREATED _____

_____

COMMENTS_____

_____

_____